## Advance Praise

"As an Interim University Executive Director of CUNY Online, and after a long career in education, including some co-authorship with James, I was pleased to see this book on the development of what is called 'professional wisdom' in college students. In higher education, the primary focus continues to be on classical knowledge transfer from faculty to students; however, we need to be cognizant that our students are living in a world outside the higher education walls and can and should learn from it as well. This book drives home that point and even does it from the perspective of how we are built with a brain that not only processes information but adds feelings from direct experiences to create value out of that information. Students gain a deeper understanding of the material because they see its relevance and utility. Abstract concepts become tangible when used to solve actual problems in workplaces or communities, and these experiences help drive students to their 'aha moment' as they pursue their interests and passion. For anyone who cares about higher education from the student perspective, this is a must-read."

—**Judith Cahn,** EdD, Interim University Executive Director, CUNY Online

"The book *Professional Wisdom* by James Stellar and Brandy Eggan hits at the core of what experiential education adds to a classical college education. As a Vice President of Cooperative Education at Drexel University, I see every day the maturity our program of experiential education brings to college students. I really like that the authors grounded that observation in basic, easy-to-understand brain facts and ideas that makes it seem more fundamental. I recommend particularly that non-cooperative education university students, faculty, and administrators read this book. It will reframe their thinking about a college education."

—**Ian Sladen,** Vice President of Cooperative Education, Drexel University

"The book that James Stellar and Brandy Eggan have written grows out of an experience James and I had together as President and Dean of the College of Arts and Sciences at Northeastern University, a cooperative education school that rose rapidly in reputation while we were in office together and continued after. *Professional Wisdom* helps explain the notable maturity we saw in our students as a result of the off-campus work experiences that were an intrinsic part of our educational program. The book extends that thinking to all higher education by pointing out the neuroscientific reasons why experiential education can significantly enhance classroom studies and thus greatly enhance student growth. I urge college-going students and families as well as higher education administrators and faculty to have a look and pay attention to these important principles."

—**Richard Freeland,** Former President, Northeastern University and former Commissioner, Massachusetts Department of Higher Education

"In today's word of holding educational institutions accountable for the value of their outcomes, students must develop the professional wisdom needed to be career or grad school ready. Institutions of higher learning and their students need to upgrade the development of professional wisdom from an occasional occurrence to an intentional outcome based on an institutional commitment. In our world, filled with an abundance of technology and rapidly emerging AI, the question is 'How can educational institutions work with their students to develop the needed level of professional wisdom?' What role does brain functioning play in bringing about professional wisdom? If you are at all curious about this, then you must read this book."

—**Richard Porter,** Past Vice President of Cooperative Education and Professor of Mathematics, Northeastern University

# PROFESSIONAL WISDOM

# PROFESSIONAL WISDOM

## What a College Student's Brain and Career Need

**JAMES R. STELLAR**
PhD

**BRANDY L. EGGAN**
PhD

IDEAPRESS
PUBLISHING

WASHINGTON, DC

IDEAPRESS
PUBLISHING

Copyright © 2025 by James R. Stellar, PhD, and Brandy L. Eggan, PhD

All rights reserved. No part of this book may be reproduced, stored, or transmitted by any means—whether auditory, graphic, mechanical, or electronic—without written permission of both publisher and author, except in the case of brief excerpts used in critical articles and reviews. Unauthorized reproduction of any part of this work is illegal and is punishable by law.

Ideapress Publishing | www.ideapresspublishing.com

All trademarks are the property of their respective companies.

Cover Design: Jenny Volvovski
Interior Design: Jessica Angerstein

Cataloging-in-Publication Data is on file with the Library of Congress.

Hardcover ISBN: 978-1-64687-204-6

**Special Sales**

Ideapress books are available at a special discount for bulk purchases for sales promotions and premiums, or for use in corporate training programs. Special editions, including personalized covers, a custom foreword, corporate imprints, and bonus content, are also available.

1 2 3 4 5 6 7 8 9 10

# Contents

Two Coauthors ................................................................. i

Acknowledgments ............................................................. v

**Preface** Professional Wisdom in College Students ............ vii

**Chapter 1** Cultivating Wisdom Through Experiential Learning in College ........................................................... 1

**Chapter 2** Two Minds in the Brain ................................... 25

**Chapter 3** How the Brain Works to Divide Implicit and Explicit Thinking ............................................................. 45

**Chapter 4** A Deeper Look at Implicit Brain Processes and Neuroplasticity .......................................................... 59

**Chapter 5** Crossing the Implicit-Explicit Threshold While Moving from Learning to Habit .............................. 75

**Chapter 6** Higher Education Structure and the Development of Professional Wisdom ............................... 95

**Chapter 7** Intelligence and How Best to Learn Inside and Outside of the Classroom ......................................... 113

**Chapter 8** Impacts of COVID-19 and Remote Learning on Professional Wisdom ................................................ 137

**Chapter 9** The Future of Higher Education in Combining Skills with Knowledge: Technology, AI, and Government ............ 157

**Chapter 10** Back to the Brain: Neocortical Re-Representation, Explicit Thinking, and Neocortical Symbolic Logic .......................... 179

**Chapter 11** What Colleges and Universities Can Do to Develop Professional Wisdom ................................................ 199

Three Final Remarks from the Authors ................................................ 215

Conclusion ........................................................................................ 219

Endnotes .......................................................................................... 221

Index ............................................................................................... 241

# Two Coauthors

Jim Stellar and Brandy Eggan are both neuroscientists who started their PhD studies working on basic mechanisms of reward in laboratory animals. Both are now college-level educators interested in making higher education work better for students after graduation while also fulfilling the historic academic mission to expand the mind. They were introduced to each other in 2016 by a colleague (not a neuroscientist) who decided that the two people who talked a lot about laboratory rats on drugs should probably get to know each other. At this time, Brandy was finishing her PhD at Albany Medical College. Jim had done that long ago, earning a PhD in 1976 at the University of Pennsylvania. Just as Brandy was graduating and looking for the next step in her academic journey, Jim was serving as the interim president at the nearby University at Albany in the State University of New York (SUNY) system. It didn't take long for these two "rat scientists" to realize their shared passions for higher education administration, understanding decision-making behavior, and helping students succeed in their academic journeys, which ultimately developed into a partnership of learning, mentoring, and getting a little bit wiser themselves along the way.

Now, a bit more about Jim. Jim is in his mid-seventies and full of experience—some might even say old (*senior* would be a polite word). He is currently a full professor of behavioral neuroscience in the Psychology Department at the University at Albany, having "retired" from senior university administration to return to the faculty to teach and write. Jim has had a long academic career, moving from his PhD to a two-year postdoctoral fellowship in the Anatomy Department at the University of Pennsylvania Medical School and then to an assistant professorship in the Psychology Department at Harvard University in 1978. After this, he moved to Northeastern University, became a full professor, and eventually became dean of the College of Arts and Sciences during the beginning of the period of the university's remarkable rise in reputation and ranking. After well over a decade at Northeastern, he then switched to the public sector, becoming provost (academic vice president) twice, first at Queens College, City University of New York (CUNY) and then at the University at Albany. After spending time moving up through the ranks to interim president, Jim returned full-time to the faculty in 2019, where he continues to teach courses in Introductory Psychology, Psychopharmacology, and Capstones in Decision-Making Behavior.

Brandy, on the other hand, is much younger, in her early thirties. After defending her PhD, she began working for Jim as a postdoctoral fellow, learning the ins and outs of university structure as well as coauthoring a book on the importance of diversity in higher education (with a neuroscience flair, of course). Brandy then transitioned to teaching Anatomy and Physiology full-time at Maria College, a private nursing college in Albany. In 2020, she moved to Siena College, where she now teaches additional courses, including Behavioral Neuroscience in the Biology and Psychology Department. She has remained a faculty member at Albany Medical College after completing her degree, where she teaches medical and graduate students and has also worked for many years as a research coordinator for New York's Science and Technology Entry Program, a state-funded program for underrepresented middle and high school students. It was work with these students as well as many research projects with underrepresented medical students that inspired her to get a graduate studies certificate in restorative justice from the University of San Diego and then a master's in restorative justice from Vermont Law School. Additionally, Brandy works as the program director of the Leadership in Medicine program at Union College, which is a unique eight-year BS–MBA–MD combined degree program, keeping her passion for teaching, administration, and research all alive.

These experiences have allowed Jim and Brandy to share a unique dynamic. Together, they run a virtual writing lab (https://neuro-exed.com) with undergraduates (no more rats). Students in this lab get to build projects based on topics they're passionate about. You can see their work in the several hundred coauthored blogs posted since 2009 on www.otherlobe.com. The underlying theme is cognitive-emotional factors in decision-making in higher education, often based on experiences like internships, something that Jim and Brandy both remain very committed to. Jim was able to combine many of the earlier blogs into his 2017 book *Education That Works*. Brandy brought her passion for diversity to this dynamic while writing the book *Diversity at College: Real Stories of Students Conquering Bias and Making Higher Education More Inclusive,* which features personal stories from current and former students. Since then, many more blog posts have emerged, as have shifts in the direction of the lab and the coauthors' desire to write about this thing they've been consistently calling "professional wisdom" for almost a decade now. And to think . . . it all began with two neuroscientists putting drugs into some rats!

# Acknowledgments

Together, we two would like to thank all of our students who helped us hatch the ideas that you see here. Two of them in particular, Rachel Orenstein and Vanessa NyBlom, worked with us on this book, giving ongoing reactions as it developed. To them we owe a particular debt of gratitude.

As partners in running our little writing lab (which is mostly virtual), we've had the pleasure of seeing many of our mentees go on to accomplish great things for themselves in college and after graduation, and we could not be prouder. We've also gone through some challenges ourselves, including Brandy's unexpected battle with advanced-stage cancer and the entire team's efforts to keep Jim from turning into an old curmudgeon. This work would not have been possible without the support from one another, our families, and our wonderful students who inspire us to keep this enthusiasm we have for blending neuroscience and higher education together. This book has come from almost a decade of nerdy conversation, passion, and collaborations with amazing people along the way.

## Preface

# Professional Wisdom in College Students

What are you going to do when you graduate from college?

Many of us are familiar with this oftentimes dreaded question that comes up for college students at family gatherings. It is the question that every parent, grandparent, aunt, uncle, and cousin seems to ask and that so many undergraduates seem to fear. In college, not only does a student have to establish a disciplinary interest in a particular major but they also have to develop a maturity in that field that will allow them to go beyond college and be a successful member of society. They must learn to be career ready. Let's call that "professional wisdom" and discuss how students get it—or at least the beginning of it.

Those of us working in higher education are very aware of this need (and arguably have been for a long time), but higher education as an institution, despite its long history, seems to only just now be realizing that this maturity (or professional wisdom) is boosted by real-world experience—and that experience is likely to come outside the classroom. Such wisdom is a good bit more than just having the marketable skills needed to start a career. We think it is a combination of intellectual and intuitive reasoning that grows out of both academic knowledge and practical application. Furthermore, we have seen a growing demand from families for better development for their children—including clearer outcomes of career success after college, which can't be accomplished by classroom learning alone. Now, with modern neuroscience that supports the importance and effectiveness of developing professional wisdom, we believe we can make the case that it is exactly what institutions need to focus on.

So how do colleges and universities do that? The answer is practically as old as civilization itself, going back to apprenticeships associated with craftspeople in ancient Babylon four thousand years ago:[1] You get it from experience. Higher education is designed to provide academic knowledge for students, as one would expect from an operation that has been refining its classroom-based approach for hundreds of years.[2] However, that is only the first step, and a student must get their hands dirty, so to say, to see how their knowledge works in the real world. This is something that most colleges and universities need to improve upon in addition to their other challenges, such as keeping up with advancements in technology. While the knowledge part thrives in higher education, the practical component suffers. Employers constantly tell our college leadership teams that our graduates are smart in terms of facts and theories but too often lack the ability to persuasively communicate and present that knowledge to others or to apply these facts and theories to the task at hand.

Today, colleges and universities do seem to recognize the value of having some programs outside the classroom, such as study-abroad trips, service-learning programs, and undergraduate research. They have nurtured those activities in the last five decades to better attract and retain students. They also know that if a student can get relevant workplace experience to complement their academic studies—through a paid or unpaid internship or even through a job—they can find out more about who they are and whether they fit within their chosen field of study. With that insight, the student more easily knows the right step to take after graduation, whether that be a job or further professional training in some type of graduate education.

We believe this trend is the beginning of higher education recognizing the importance of professional wisdom. In our opinion, colleges and universities ought to strive to encourage and facilitate this growth rather than just leave it as something a student often does largely on their own. We think career exploration should start at the beginning of a college education and not toward the end, when we typically see far too many students visiting their college's career office for the first time. A taste of this real-world application makes students better consumers of the academic knowledge presented in the classroom. It certainly helps them succeed when they graduate. Remember the old adage of alumni: "If I knew then what I know now. . . ." Well, here is a way to get some of that wisdom while the students are still in attendance at college.

Of course, there are books about skills and learning from experience in place of or in addition to higher education. Two recent examples are *Apprentice Nation* and *The Career Arts*.[3,4] They contain important conversations about higher education and potential supplements or alternatives to its structure. But that is not our book. Our book is about the student and the development of some professional wisdom while they are still in the cloister of a college education. This book discusses how experiential education impacts a student's motivation and choices, which has a firm basis in neuroscience and is supported by decades of research on physical changes in the brain. It is also about the various opportunities colleges and universities have (or should have) to help their students develop professional wisdom without compromising but rather enhancing the basic mission of expanding the student's mind. Our approach is unique in that it explores the fundamental roots of decision-making and learning, applies them to the current undergraduate learner, and evaluates potential avenues for change in the current practices of higher education.

We chose the title *Professional Wisdom* to allow us to do two things. First, we do not want to disrespect the classic role of higher education in promoting the life of the mind by going deep into disciplinary knowledge, and by promoting the excellence of thought, the innovation of ideas, and the development of important critical thinking. Second, we wanted to cultivate the notion that learning from experience is brain-natural and thereby strongly complements these classic higher education goals, particularly where they lead to careers. It also works in classical academic fields ranging from philosophy to history to mathematics. It gives the student a bit more maturity in studying those fields while in college and challenges one to think about their future career while immersed in the daily classroom environment. We hope to convince our readers of the importance of developing professional wisdom in our current and future students in higher education. It will not only create a stronger, more professional and prepared workforce but also encourage them to find their own career, one that fits—that challenges, engages, and fulfills their needs.

The brain basis behind all of this begins with our idea that meaningful and repeated work experiences with a profession, accompanied by some reflection, allows most college students to begin developing this kind of professional maturity. It may even translate to maturity in general. We believe that this professional development is due to the integration of cognitive knowledge in a brain area called the neocortex, which houses our symbolic reasoning. When that abstract cognitive knowledge mixes with another kind of felt knowledge held in lower brain levels (in the motor or limbic system), without our active thought, it gives us a gut-level evaluation of whether or not that field is right for us. As you will learn in this book, the conscious, cognitive level supports things like language, visualization, and imagination. However, to have that knowledge truly flow in someone, it must be integrated with knowledge gained from lower, often unconscious brain systems developed when those ideas are put into practice.

If you have ever been on a hiring committee, as we have, you know that employers seek to understand whether a job applicant has maturity or professional wisdom. If they do, they are judged to be more employable. Everyone can tell very quickly when a colleague has it. It is what we think Robert M. Pirsig referred to in his famous 1974 book *Zen and the Art of Motorcycle Maintenance*, when he wrote these simple words: "the mechanic's feel."[5] It is what we think Oscar Wilde called out in the negative in his play *Lady Windermere's Fan,* when the character Lord Darlington said a cynic is someone "who knows the price of everything and the value of nothing."[6] Higher education does not want to graduate students who are cynics. They want to graduate the student who is more mature, desirable, and employable because they have a feel for their chosen career. That is a student who has the beginning of professional wisdom.

## Chapter 1
# Cultivating Wisdom Through Experiential Learning in College

Let's start with a fundamental question. How does higher education cultivate professional wisdom for its students?

In addition to wanting our students to be wiser, academia has some obligation to help students acquire a greater understanding of potential career paths. So, the answer to the question is simple: help them go beyond the classroom for relevant, hands-on experience. There, they can put that good academic knowledge to work and see how it feels. We would also argue that it is brain-natural, particularly if you believe as we do that everyone has both a heart and a head that learn to love something. In this case, we hope it is a lifelong career path.

Letting students step off campus to gain experience sounds simple, but it is a challenge for colleges and universities. First, it opposes the structure and centuries of tradition that say higher education institutions should take care of their students, similar to that old Latin phrase *in loco parentis* (in lieu of the parents) that was widely used when our much older author, Jim, went to college. That approach may have worked before the information revolution, back when almost all knowledge was held by colleges and universities, but change is needed now that information is at a student's fingertips on any laptop or smartphone. Artificial intelligence (AI) has further exacerbated knowledge accessibility, as it can put together summaries or stories about knowledge that make it look (or sort of look) like a human did it when all the human did was copy and paste a professor's prompt into an AI website.

Also, the marketplace for a college or university is now specifically asking for improved employment outcomes in response to the investment of time and money that the student and their family will make.[1] Brandy passes a large visual reminder of this every day on her way into campus as the welcome banner flashes, "The Number One College in the State for Job Placement After Graduation."[2] Worse yet, Jim passes every day a college that closed within the last two years because of the financial pressure of too few students after more than one hundred years of operation.[3] More and more, we see the market shift its values away from the "ivory tower" justification developed by centuries of refinement, accreditation, and past expectations about what happens at a college or university. The shift is toward practical experiences plus that old ivory tower in an equation that could potentially create some professionally wise graduates.

To go a bit deeper, that classic ivory tower formulation includes those specific classes that fit into a college major and eventually other degree requirements like general education courses, minors, and electives. It includes the fact that every individual course has a syllabus that shows the topic of the day, the dates of the exams, how the grade will be determined, and so on. It is all very fair, standard, effective, and highly predictable. It is not like the turbulent, authentic, and compelling world outside of higher education. What is even more odd to an educator who has worked at a cooperative education university that is itself more than one hundred years old is how there is no real loss to higher education learning from weaving work-based learning and other such experiences into the college years. In fact, we argue that it makes students academically better and much more competitive for the job market while they are in college as well as after they graduate. It confers a beginning of the development of professional wisdom that supplements both their academic studies as well as their potential career path.

Look at it from the other side. When a college student starts an internship, the experience is often unpredictable, as the student is entering that job the first time. For many, it isn't just their first time in *that* job, but their first time having a job (or even something that looks like a job) at all. Because of this factor, the experience retains an element of spontaneity. Real-world activities often enter the workplace without warning, which the work team must handle or otherwise serious consequences could ensue—much more serious than getting a poor grade on an exam in a course. As we said, many alumni have told us they wished they knew in college what they know now, years after graduation. Luckily for current college students, this kind of experiential activity is exactly how to get some of that knowledge before moving out into the workforce or into a graduate education.

Now more than ever it is our job as those working in higher education to tell our students to get out of the classroom, which might seem counterintuitive. We have a responsibility to encourage them to do an internship, or volunteer, or shadow, or study abroad, or work with a professor on their research. These and other experiences are going to help students to determine that all-important fit with the potential career, and they will shape the student's academic knowledge into an emerging professional wisdom.

## Cooperative Education Programs: A Lesson from the Most Substantial Type of Internship

Cooperative education specializes in developing practical experience alongside classroom learning. It was established over one hundred years ago when a young engineering professor at the University of Cincinnati named Herman Schneider had an unusual idea for how to enhance the classical engineering education that students received from their university.[4] He thought that students would better understand the point of classroom lessons and actually learn more if they had periods of industry-based work in between periods of classroom study. The University of Cincinnati board of trustees gave him a year to try it out, and to everyone's surprise, it was so successful that they quickly adopted it as their core university structure. Schneider himself ultimately became the university's president.[5]

A few years after Cincinnati started cooperative education, Northeastern University in Boston and Drexel University in Philadelphia both adopted the same basic model. The schools partnered with outside entities to offer workplace opportunities as experiential learning. It was a major departure for the operation of a college, which typically featured a cloistered environment, much like the monasteries from which they developed long ago. These three major American universities have now had cooperative education programs for more than a century, with many other colleges and universities and specific programs following suit in America and around the world.

Jim knows the cooperative education system well, having been both a professor and dean of the College of Arts and Sciences at Northeastern University for twenty-two years and having more recently served on the board and executive committee for the World Association of Cooperative Education, now known as WACE.[6] At Northeastern and any cooperative education school, full-time, paid internships or cooperative education often produces a much higher degree of engagement in students than if they were to focus on studies alone. Cooperative education experiences are serious work. If the experience seems productive to the student, that seriousness rubs off. It was very common to hear at Northeastern that students left the campus for their first cooperative education experience at age nineteen and came back six months later at age twenty-five. The change in the students was undeniable.

Part of the reason for this trend was that a full-time, paid internship, even for just one academic term, is the closest thing a college student can have to a real job. Failure on the job means being fired; do-overs and asking a boss to take an assignment past a deadline are not options. This is a huge shift from the classroom setting, where we often see makeup exams and other bonus assignments to earn credit so that all students have an option to pass the course despite not hitting the requirements written in the syllabus (which in this case we would look at as the job contract). For students struggling with time management, they are often referred to an academic support office or similar resource where they can work with others to develop those skills. In the workforce, this person would likely wind up in a less-than-supportive human resources office having a stern conversation with extreme consequences, such as immediate termination. Failure to succeed in business placements would disrupt people's lives. Nothing seems to concentrate the mind more than the prospect of success versus failure in the real world.

Every working adult lives with that pressure, but it is just not true for many college students who operate within the safe cocoon of higher education. If they have jobs, it is often to supplement their finances rather than sustain them. All college students need to figure out who they are or who they will be professionally, which is admittedly a challenging task. In our experience, students know that. They understand what is coming after graduation and that they will ultimately have to work to support themselves and possibly a family. With that in mind, they plan to find a career that pays them well enough to live in a level of comfort. College is supposed to be a wonderful opportunity for students to learn facts and theories, to safely test out ideas for fields they want to pursue, and to grow socially with their peers; that is its strength. But serious career exploration through experiential learning is largely missing or is considered only at the end of college, when students typically start to look for that next step after graduation. Unfortunately, such students also lack the professional wisdom that employers want and that could have been layered on top of academic learning. The good news is that all of this is now changing with societal and even governmental interests, as you will see in later chapters of this book.

So, what is happening in a cooperative education school that is different, and why is it so impactful? In a cooperative education college or university, almost everyone is dedicated to blending classwork with a paid internship. Some institutions, like Northeastern University, work in a six-month alternating fashion that gives students up to three full-time employment opportunities in the five years of their undergraduate experience required for graduation. Others, like Drexel University, currently feature somewhat shorter work terms, as they operate on the quarter-term schedule. The length of the term arrangement does not seem to matter, though many higher education institutions have converted to semesters from quarters. Regardless, what we do know is that upon graduation, almost all undergraduates with cooperative education experience are able to land a job, oftentimes immediately after or even before graduating. For others, they typically find a position within a few months. Those pursuing acceptance to graduate school or a professional program also are extremely successful. It is so popular that in schools without cooperative education programs, full-time summer internships as well as part-time internships during the academic year are now emerging more and more widely. Unfortunately, many of these internships are not paid like cooperative education programs, but the results are still somewhat similar and students are increasingly aware that they benefit from them.

*Are cooperative education students actually wiser upon graduation?* That remains to be seen, but they certainly have a documented skill set allowing reflection upon how academic knowledge and critical thinking intersect with the skills and felt experiences of a working field. Employers have a crying need for this combination of knowledge and skill, and they are not shy about stating it today. We think a major change is washing over all higher education institutions the way other experiential programs already have in the form of study abroad and undergraduate research opportunities. It used to be said that without reasonable housing, food, and academic advising, colleges and universities would run into enrollment problems. Now, they need these internship, study abroad, undergraduate research, and even community service programs to attract enough students in the first place to meet their enrollment goals. In serving on admissions panels at our colleges and universities, experiences outside of the classroom are one of the first things that prospective students ask questions about. If that school does not have a great answer, they will not succeed.

Over the last fifty years (not a long time for higher education and its centuries-old history), we have seen an increasing number of students, families, and employers clamoring for an education that will not only inform and enlighten but also provide students with the skills needed to succeed after graduation. In addition to the four years of typical time investment, the cost now reaches more than $1.7 trillion in combined student debt in America.[7] Thus, the justification for college must be high, and it does really help if one can get a well-paying job upon graduation to capitalize on the personal growth achieved.

The majority of our undergraduate learners do not attend a cooperative education school though, as these programs are extremely competitive and there just are not enough programs available at this time. *In that case, how does the regular (non–cooperative education) college build their students' real-world experience?*

## A Quick Review of the Other Types of Experiential Activities

In recent years, the higher education industry has developed other kinds of experiential activities in addition to cooperative education programs. Many are now pervasive across colleges and universities. As previously mentioned, it is very likely that students would not attend without such programs. With too many institutions going bankrupt and closing their doors these days for lack of enrollment, that is an important motivator.

**Internships** have a few key differences that set them apart from cooperative education, though they are both forms of experiential learning that provide students with practical experience in their fields. First off, cooperative education work experience is typically paid. That makes a difference to the employer who wants to get their money's worth out of the student's work, and so the experience is often more substantial than an unpaid internship. Second, cooperative education is typically well integrated into the college curriculum, with preparation courses and a reflection activity when the student returns. They can also be longer, sometimes even lasting multiple semesters. On the other hand, internships typically take place over the summer or during semester breaks, when competition from other internship programs is high.

Cooperative education experiences are typically more structured and almost always in the field of a student's academic program, whereas internships can be shorter, less structured, and more exploratory. This gives cooperative education the ability to better integrate academic learning with practical work experience in a way that allows for reflection and critical thinking. In non–cooperative education colleges or universities, reflection often isn't the primary focus of an internship, but rather it prioritizes networking and getting a feel for whether the work area is a good personal fit.

There is an important question as to whether or not an internship earns credits even with legal implications in terms of free labor,[8] but we will leave that to the accrediting bodies and higher education systems to sort out. More recently, colleges are developing credit-bearing internship programs, with some offering opportunities to receive general education credits that could improve reflection and what the students take out of the experience, but these are run quite differently across undergraduate institutions at this time.[9]

Some specific internship programs require mandatory time commitments and may even be integrated into curricular requirements for specific programs. Often, they are in medical areas such as undergraduate nursing programs, where a specific number of experiential clinical hours are mandated by accrediting bodies. Also, remember that primary and secondary education programs have long featured a practicum where teachers-in-training in college work with education professionals. These internship-based experiences capture some of the elements of a full-time, paid cooperative education, particularly as they are tied much more to the institution than when a student finds such an opportunity on their own.

A faculty member staying in communication with the student while they are on a credit-bearing internship can be good in terms of integrating academic learning with the experience. In our nursing programs, the faculty member is side-by-side with the student as they learn hands-on at the bedside, not only for safety but also to give the benefit of a direct oversight. In less hands-on experiences and internships, though, it can be bad in the sense that the student still feels like they are in college even though they are at a worksite, especially if the internship is part-time and learning and skill development aren't a focus of the experience. The bottom line is that there are many ways to do an internship, and outside organizations like the National Association of Colleges and Employers (NACE) take a serious interest in them.[10]

We note here that it is a little different when the cooperative education student is a paid employee and the employer is utilizing them in this way. Here it helps if the college or university stays away so that the student can have the full employment experience. If that does not happen, it is a little better if the college or university takes a serious role in helping the student get the internship or helps them understand its implications after. Perhaps the least beneficial arrangement is when the student just gets the internship on their own because they know it is important. Of course, we would never object to any student getting any relevant workplace or growth-driving experience as long as it is informative.

**Undergraduate research** is also an excellent way for a student to earn some hands-on experience and take a step toward cultivating professional wisdom. More specifically, undergraduate research refers to academic or scientific research projects conducted as part of university studies. Oftentimes students hear the word "research" and think that they can only work in a science lab, such as that of a biologist or a chemist doing benchwork with beakers and test tubes. This impression is reinforced by undergraduate research that really began with roots in the STEM (science, technology, engineering, and math) fields, with the federal US National Science Foundation currently supporting over six thousand students annually.[11] Undergraduate research projects of all types allow students to delve into any subject area of interest under the guidance of a faculty member. We have seen how this experience has worked well in all fields and is often built into college honors programs in all fields. Today, perhaps a social work major completes a semester of fieldwork and assesses their patients' responses to a new treatment plan, a creative arts major does a short documentary about diversity initiatives on campus, or a history major does a literature review on Middle East conflicts throughout the past thirty years—all examples that could fall under the umbrella of undergraduate research.

Engaging in these creative projects regardless of the form provides undergraduates with valuable hands-on experience in their field of study, allowing them to apply theoretical knowledge learned in the classroom to real-world problems or questions. Aside from helping students decide if they want to enter that field, it also helps them to develop critical thinking, problem-solving, and research skills as well as collaboration and communication skills. At the Massachusetts Institute of Technology, the Undergraduate Research Opportunities Program (UROP) has been around for well over fifty years. In 2023, more than 90 percent of its students were participating in undergraduate research.[12] If one looks a little deeper, this activity goes back to the early nineteenth century, when some German universities began undergraduate research practices.

While it is reportedly a challenge for students to find exactly what they are interested in doing for undergraduate research, these experiences undeniably enhance the student's academic experience, prepare them for future graduate studies or careers, and may even lead to opportunities for publication or conference presentations. Many universities actively encourage undergraduate research through dedicated programs or in summer research activities, and many have expos or showcases where students can present their research. The Council on Undergraduate Research is a national organization that represents this work and holds an annual national conference.[13] Many disciplinary research societies have dedicated groups within them that also support undergraduate research. In our field, with the Society for Neuroscience,[14] this work falls to Faculty for Undergraduate Neuroscience (with the creative acronym FUN).[15] The work itself, the mentoring by a faculty member, the emphasis of what amounts to real-world production in the research world—all of it contributes to the development of professional wisdom, and that can happen anywhere faculty who do research meet students who want to participate.

**Service-learning** has an even older tradition within higher education than undergraduate research, perhaps beginning in America with the Morrill Act of the late nineteenth century, which formed the public university system that today educates most of America's college students.[16] A public university has the same two basic roles of knowledge generation (research) and knowledge dissemination (teaching) as any university, but these two roles are accompanied by a serious third role of serving the community that helps to support them with tax dollars. Of course, private universities also like to maintain good relations with the community, but given the taxpayer funding of the public university, it is much more built in for them.

The basic concept of service-learning fits with much of what we have already written about experiential education and has national representation in AmeriCorps and other organizations.[17] Almost every college or university has some kind of service center on their campus, and students take seriously the idea of giving back to the community. As discussed before, the learning takes place out of the classroom environment through direct service, although some colleges or universities have specific service-learning courses where this activity is like a laboratory exercise that occurs within the course structure.

Notice the hyphen between the words "service" and "learning" in this term: that is no accident of history or convention. At least since the publication of a book by Jacoby and Associates in 1996, the field strives for the interaction between service and learning, and current practitioners insist on that integration.[18] The idea here is to go beyond the good work that students naturally want to do or the way most colleges and universities want to be of service to their communities (even if they are not publicly funded) to integrate the learning with the service. To us, the hyphen also emphasizes the idea of students reflecting upon their service, in part to better extract that learning from the experience. As we will explore later, reflection is a big part of the theory about what turns experiential activities into learning, but it also fits with our broad view of the need to integrate the emotional impact of the experience with the cognitive thinking the student has about what they plan to study or become after graduation.

Service-learning can come in various forms. It doesn't have to be participation in a social justice initiative or community service organization. Two of the most basic forms of service-learning we see in our undergraduate communities are peer tutoring and serving as an orientation leader for an incoming class of students. More developed service-learning projects sometimes receive credit, are integrated into a course, or are required within a curriculum. Brandy works at a Franciscan college—service is part of their mission and a top priority for students. The college partners with the Bonner Foundation,[19] an organization currently working with many universities to incorporate service-learning into their curriculums by sponsoring not only opportunities for service but also funding for students and academic credit.[20] Programs like this seem like a win-win for the student and the university, falling in line with the mission, teaching students reciprocity in a hands-on environment, promoting civic engagement while fostering relationships between the school and community, and also contributing to positive social change. While these programs are optional in undergraduate institutions, graduate schools (including our many medical schools) require significant hours of service-learning as a mandatory component of medical education. This makes sense when you think about the important role these future doctors will have in their communities and their choice to practice in underserved areas. Places of higher education are shifting to include administrative positions solely focused on establishing and maintaining these community partnerships and supporting students. People holding these roles know that the process is important and delicate and requires some good old-fashioned matchmaking.[21]

**Study abroad** programs are so popular that they have become practically a requirement for colleges and universities to attract students. Their history is as old as cooperative education, about one hundred years, and they have evolved from a primarily language/culture learning function into a way to prepare students for life and work in a globalized society (evident in its current level of travel and internet connectivity).[22] Like the other areas discussed earlier, there are national organizations that promote studying abroad.[23] Many universities have specific institutions with which they partner, and some even have outposts in foreign countries so that students can attend there but still be nominally in their home institutions. Some professors are also extremely passionate about immersive cultural learning and choose to create their own faculty-led trips to destinations they find best fitting. Sometimes, study abroad is incorporated into internships or work experiences. In most modern large businesses and even some smaller workplaces, we see significant international operations for American students. Business schools often have international business majors, and to meet this need, they maintain special opportunities and even accreditation for these abroad programs.[24] In almost all colleges, study abroad is seen as an experiential opportunity that leads to a greater perspective on oneself, one's country, and the world.

We note that studying abroad is not a vacation, as some like to say. With entire centers and multiple staff members and student workers devoted to this at some institutions, living abroad for the semester and being out of the student's normal comfort zone can have a big impact on their overall maturity that goes beyond getting a new perspective on their home country or learning a new language. A structured study abroad program at another university in another country with other undergraduates of one's own age offers opportunities that go beyond simple travel (particularly with their families) or exposure within their home institution to international students, or even students from a diverse ethnic background. Full immersion into a university with everything you would expect—courses at specific times, exams, and homework—is just one option we see our undergraduate study abroad offices offering.

As mentioned, some universities offer unique faculty-led trips to areas they are passionate about, such as a biology professor studying a specific type of moss that is only found in one tropical location of the world or a historian studying French military history and bringing their students to France to explore the historic libraries firsthand. Some institutions even offer solo trips without academic structure, where a student could find themselves at perhaps a site for a public water drilling in a third-world country, aiding in the design process as it fits in line with their civil engineering studies.

It's not hard to see that studying abroad varies in structures and outcomes, even blending different forms of experiential learning such as service along with an international experience. We think that what is important is the immersion where the student is the outsider in so many aspects of college life, while still having the familiar framework of courses, service, or internship hours, just somewhere new. Regardless of whether this full-semester or week-long travel is within the major or is credit-bearing, it is not uncommon for students to seek out the opportunity for personal growth, professional development, networking opportunities, and ultimately a unique cultural experience that can enrich the college community upon the student's return. Another win-win for the student and the school. It is also another potential opportunity for cognitive-emotional integration, where reflection can lead to elements of growth in professional wisdom.

## A Few Other Forms of Experiential Learning

There are many other types of learning from experiences. Some of them are even integrated with the classroom structure. Some majors, such as social work and education, have courses that require committed community partners. Special courses here are designed to give students the opportunity to enhance academic learning about a topic like dealing with social problems (such as homelessness or public health issues) while actually researching within a specific community. Students in these programs typically have a designated amount of contact hours for the course that are dedicated to community immersion, and they have dedicated classroom time where they bring back the information they are learning in their communities. Opportunities such as these require extensive work and time associated with developing these partnerships, and they often have an administrative coordinator assigned to developing and maintaining them.

At one of our institutions, for example, there is a public health immersion course that allows students to spend a semester studying a community in South America through literature and virtual communications. For the community-immersed element of the course, students then travel to the site for one to two weeks and attempt to improve the public health of that community. One semester, the needs assessment revealed a lack of access to proper preventative dental hygiene items. The school held a fundraiser to collect the items, the students developed informational brochures about proper dental hygiene in the community's native language, and then the students traveled there to work with the community to address this need. Other years focused on access to feminine hygiene products, proper diet, blood pressure monitoring, cardiovascular health, and more. Most importantly, all these projects were student led, fostering leadership and cultural competency while developing their maturity and empathy along the way.

Another interesting, more recent development has been a project called collaborative online international learning (or COIL) that was started at the State University of New York central office about twenty years ago. COIL involves two classes with two professors tackling a combined project.[25] The key is that one of the two classes is international, creating at times intense interactions between the students. The collaborative projects and discussions, enhanced by the student-focused design, drive students through virtual collaboration to become globally engaged. COIL gives participating schools a cost-effective way to provide students with a meaningful opportunity for global interaction built right into their programs of study. At this point, COIL has reached about 150 different institutions.

## Career Services Offices

Before leaving this topic of learning from experience, we want to briefly mention career services offices. They seem to be the right place to organize workplace experiences in a student's field of study. Such offices have hard-working staff and often succeed in connecting students to internships or summer job opportunities. But too often these experiences are happening in the latter years of a college education, when students are finally thinking about what they will do after graduation. When it comes to earlier opportunities, in our experience, most students are doing it for themselves or come from a household of highly educated parents that are working side-by-side with the student on their search. Earnest career offices would love to provide these early experiences and can do much more than a quick, panicked stop near graduation. So why don't they?

One need only compare career services with classical cooperative education programs to see the weakness: institutional investment. For example, the three original cooperative education programs mentioned at the beginning of this chapter (at the University of Cincinnati, Northeastern University, and Drexel University) invest perhaps five times as much in their cooperative education programs as non–cooperative education universities invest in their career services. Actual numbers vary, but as an example, at the University at Albany, the Office of Career Development[26] is fairly typical, having about ten people servicing more than twelve thousand students. Meanwhile, at Northeastern University, they have more than fifty cooperative education coordinators university-wide for about fifteen thousand undergraduates. Perhaps that is why cooperative education at Northeastern is much more a part of the overall college education program and culture. Institutions, like individuals, tend to value what they pay for.

## Summary

Experiential practices are integrated in some majors. Often, business and engineering schools have such experiences built into their programs and cultures. They typically involve practicing members of the field to contribute to the undergraduate's education through participation in seminars, workshops, and capstone courses. In medical fields such as nursing or speech pathology, undergraduate students must meet national accrediting standards for required clinical hours prior to sitting for a licensing exam. It makes sense: Who among us wants to have a licensed health care provider who has never had their hands on a patient or stood at a bedside? A question is whether participants in these programs are professionally wiser than others or just have a needed skill set. Given our belief that experiential education taps into a brain-natural kind of learning that complements classroom learning, we do think they are professionally wiser. We will come back to that later.

Now that we have briefly surveyed the field, we would like to shift gears a bit to discuss the neuroscience behind this development of professional wisdom before we talk about ways to cultivate this in our undergraduate learners.

Chapter 2

# Two Minds in the Brain

How did we humans come to develop a college education with an overwhelming focus on cognitive content knowledge, largely from classes? More important to this book, how did we mostly leave out a key component of skills and mastery that comes from accompanying direct experience?

The answer to these questions lies in the natural bias we all have toward the cognitive part of ourselves as individuals, given the way our brains are built. Our educational systems are a reflection of the rational, logical self-view of who we are—not that such a view makes the structure of our institutions right.

We perceive ourselves as the unitary rational thinker in our head. It is an overwhelmingly compelling perception. And many of our institutions are implicitly based on it. There is one person in our head. Our internal speech is our own, and it is based on how we interpret our environment. We are in charge, even if we have some impulses that we sometimes struggle to control. Therefore, it just makes sense for a college or university to focus on rational knowledge—so-called facts and theories—and meanwhile let others, perhaps in the apprentice-based trades, teach how it feels to apply that knowledge.

That is not quite true in reality, however. That is not really who we are. We know this from modern neuroscience, particularly from tools that allow scientists to create pictures of activity in the brain as it is happening in real time. We will discuss that later. For now, you need to know that unlike the chips in your computer that are synchronized by a clock, each neuron in your brain can "talk" at once, and they do. They talk to the billions of other neurons in your brain—an astounding eighty-six billion, according to current estimates.[1] Despite advances in the fields of parallel processing in computer science and AI, nothing that humans have ever built comes close to having eighty-six billion parallel processing units. Worse yet, those neurons are operating in a system with network characteristics that we do not yet understand. Some even question the use of the words "information processing" when referring to people.[2] From our perspective as neuroscientists, it is just amazing that we function at all.

Shattering the belief in the one rational voice in the head is what many think made Sigmund Freud famous—especially his ideas about the power of the unconscious in treating clinical conditions. Before him, philosopher David Hume said that "reason is, and ought only to be, the slave of the passions."[3] Antonio Damasio, a modern cognitive neurologist, wrote a book promoting the power of emotions in conscious decisions called *Descartes' Error*.[4] While he was not the first to think this way, his work was stunning at the time to a lingering era of rationalism. Much more recently, this role for emotion is what we think helped Daniel Kahneman, a Princeton University psychologist and professor, win the Nobel Prize in Economics in 2002, and it is what popularized his 2011 book *Thinking, Fast and Slow*.[5] Kahneman's decision-making psychology work explained how bubbles occur in the stock market when rational economic theory predicts they should not be there. After all, if we all really are rational economic actors that some say we are, and if there are many of us participating in setting the current stock price by buying and selling from each other, then the price should be pretty close to the predictions under the current economic conditions at that time. Yet bubbles occur. Until Kahneman, these bubbles were simply called anomalies.

The key for us here in Kahneman's book is the "thinking fast" part, or what he calls "system 1." This system is the always-on, intuitive, gut-level factor in decision-making and also goes by "heuristics" or "the rule of thumb." Often it is very useful, particularly in complex decision-making where one does not have all the information and must act quickly. But it can also bias decisions. For example, if all of your friends are buying a particular stock, you will feel the pull of buying it too because of your intuitive self and what some call "FOMO," or the fear of missing out.

This intuitive bias can happen before you even look at the profit and loss and other documents about that company. For those studying documents, you use your deliberative, calculating, rational system, what Kahneman calls "system 2," to study the company. Your rational goal is to see if its stock really has enough value to make an investment. There are other interesting examples of how heuristics help us and lead us into biases such as the anchoring effect, where a single number can anchor your guesstimate about something like the price of a car or a house, or the concept of availability bias—when something comes easily to mind and is therefore felt to be true regardless of its factual basis. Here we point out that such system 1 and system 2 thinking goes into one's decision to pick a college, a major, and a field that could become a career. It seems silly to plan a career in college only on what Kahneman would call system 2 when system 1 also exists. (For more on this, we refer you to an article titled "Two Brains Running."[6])

With the illusion of rationality so prevalent in us, it is natural for higher education to also try to be rational. After centuries of refinement, academic learning and its rational justification have become the bastion of higher education and, importantly, the business of modern college and university accreditation. We pointed that out in the previous chapter, but here we want to concentrate on the other part: the intuitive one. Another famous author, Malcolm Gladwell, referred to this as "thin slicing" in his book *Blink: The Power of Thinking Without Thinking*.[7] In college education, much of the intuitive parts of the process for the student have been weeded out. Instead, this intuitive part of learning is too often left to extracurriculars like clubs, social activities, learning from peers, or the kinds of experiential approaches discussed in the previous chapter. As you will see, we think that is wrong, and we are optimistic about the slow but steady changes we see happening now in higher education to incorporate this intuitive or emotional type of learning into the educational process. We think Kahneman and others were right and that basic neuroscience supports that dual rational-intuitive view is just brain-natural. Even Blaise Pascal, way back in the 1600s, wrote about heart and head reasons, famously saying, "Le cœur a ses raisons que la raison ne connaît point," or in English, "The heart has its reasons, which reason knows nothing of."[8] Modern neuroscience backs up Pascal, which we will detail later in the book.

For now, in college, some say that we have to educate the whole student, and we take that to mean going beyond the rational mind of facts and theories learned in the classroom. We have to educate the heart, or what we neuroscientists would call the limbic system. We, and others, think it plays a large role in helping us figure out the value of things, particularly whether they are good for us or not. When, for example, a student goes out on a paid internship in what they think might be their chosen field and comes back to college full of passion for that field, we would say that student has been educated implicitly (the heart, perhaps system 1) and has learned explicitly (the head, perhaps system 2) about the facts and theories that could well have been discussed in the classroom. We believe this type of education is brain-natural, and we will discuss this further in the following chapter. Also, importantly, we say again that this combination of academic and experiential learning can bring a student to the beginning of developing professional wisdom. By now you may be tired of us saying that. But some things bear repeating.

## Decision-Making and the Future of Happiness

Confucius and later others are supposed to have said something along the lines of "If you love what you do then you never work a day in your life." This is the essence of why we want college students to try something before they commit to a long academic career in a particular field or just jump headfirst into working in an industry.

To talk about another area where psychologists have done work that applies here, everyone thinks about what makes us happy. In a sense, it is why a student goes to college in the first place: to find out what field they should study, what they should become. We hear this a lot in college, where a student will say, "My mother thinks I should be a lawyer because I argue with her all the time." So, that student selects a major that could ultimately lead to admission to law school, and they take courses in a variety of fields that relate to the law and society. Another student's father observes they are good with numbers and suggests they should be an accountant. For some students it starts even younger, as we all probably know someone who's said, "When I grow up, I want to be a firefighter," or maybe a doctor, teacher, or the president of the United States. While that dream changes for many along the way, in that moment our self-reflective student is choosing something that makes sense to them. And it makes sense to them because, in some way, it makes them happy.

Given that both of us are neuroscientists, we do a lot of advising in the premedical area. Here the pressure is often high, particularly if one is interested in the path to medical school. The courses are demanding, the competition can be intense, and students often learn that while they have a dream of becoming a doctor, they might not do so well in biology and chemistry classes freshman year. This kind of evaluation of future happiness on the basis of reactions to courses is very common in college and often leads to some serious reevaluations. Of course, particularly in the medical field, everyone seems to know that admission into a medical school program demands some direct, internship-type experience, often facilitated by the premedical office, advisors, career centers, and so on. A 4.0 GPA may look nice on paper and show that a student is academically ready to enter a medical program, but medicine in particular is unique in that experience is required to move forward. There is a rigorous clinical component that must be met before sitting for the licensing exam. While sometimes it is the rigorous coursework that drives students to reassess their future plans, we also see that when a student gets to that hands-on setting and they just do not like it, they know that a future at the bedside would be an agonizing career choice. Or they have the opposite experience and come back and tell us that this field is really for them. So, how do we judge our future happiness? The answer is not as simple as one might expect.

Professor Dan Gilbert of Harvard argues in his book *Stumbling on Happiness* that future happiness is often misestimated. In a 2004 TED Talk,[9] he opens with a tale of someone with great fortune (winning the lottery) and misfortune (becoming a paraplegic). We all think the former would obviously result in much greater happiness a year later, but the data shows that both people in these examples are just about as happy as they were before the fortune or the misfortune. People in this situation appear to have adapted to their circumstances over the course of the year. Gilbert goes on to argue that we have an imagination machine in our heads, the prefrontal cortex, which projects what we will feel with certain outcomes. So, one would think this device would keep the fortunate person at a persistent emotional high and the opposite for he who experienced the misfortune. What we actually see, though, is that what he calls a "simulation in the head" is not really the case. Adaptation brings us back to our previous baseline.

Now, it is not our point here to discuss happiness, although every undergraduate we have met tells us that they want a college major and career that will make them happy. It's either that or to "make a lot of money." But we're lumping those two responses together because they go hand in hand in many of our students' minds. Our point here is that this process needs some grounding in the real world, where students can learn from direct interaction with their fields. This way they can learn at a cognitive level and use that simulation to imagine a bright future for themselves. That vision is important for keeping a student motivated in their career path. Keeping that vision alive is now more than ever requiring experiences outside of the traditional academic classroom. Happiness can be strongly swayed by learning at the limbic system (or emotional) level. Oftentimes gut decisions or emotional responses are what truly concrete a major decision, like selecting a college discipline. We believe that for this motivated decision-making to happen, our students are going to need some limbic learning.

## The Brain Learns Everywhere in Its Circuitry

One of the basic tenets of neuroscience is the idea of neuroplasticity. That means that each of the billions of neurons in your head and spinal cord can change their connectivity with other neurons based on its own "experience" with inputs. Of course, neurons do not think. One needs a whole brain for that. But they do change the amount of communication they have with other neurons in whatever circuit in which they are located. The formation of habit and memory are products of how neural circuits in the brain change, which can happen in any circuit. That means that the brain can learn everywhere—in the circuits that explicitly underlie your conscious thinking and processing and in the unconscious brain circuits that affect gut-feeling motivation and decision-making. This is why you feel more comfortable in the second or third week of an internship than you did in the first week. Yes, you have acquired some cognitive knowledge by that point, like knowing exactly how long it takes to get from your house to the office front door, which roads to turn on, and where the most likely spot is to find parking, but you also have begun to really develop a *feel* for the place.

To make this point in an extreme way, Jim was taught in graduate school about an experiment where a researcher had dissected the leg and controlling leg nerve ganglion out of a cockroach. The leg was hung so that the foot would dangle into a salt-water bath that was charged with electricity. What they observed was that the isolated leg nerve "learned" to hold up its foot to keep itself out of that electric bath. If the isolated leg nerve of a cockroach can learn without being at all attached to a brain, what do you think is going on when we put an entire body together through your spinal cord, or brain stem, or limbic system, or other places outside your conscious awareness?

Athletes know that they have developed a skill. Maintaining, perfecting, and advancing that skill requires practice. So do musicians. Your more musically inclined, clarinet-playing coauthor Brandy knows that teaching Jim how to play would require much more than a ten-step guide. Even a one-hundred-step guide may not get him to accurately play "Mary Had a Little Lamb" without producing awful screeching sounds. One will not truly master the beautiful tone and skillful art of playing an instrument without getting that feel for it. This is of course an extremely different kind of learning than giving someone a ten-step guide to something and asking them to memorize it. Depending on the number of words and the student's efficiency in study habits, it might be quite simple for them to deliver that guide back word-for-word an hour later on a test, but we fear for the ears of the listeners of that clarinet player's first recital. Similar to learning to ride a bicycle, what we usually see is a parent giving their child an explanation (like a lecture) on what to do, but rarely does that work. You have to let them practice and develop those lower-level brain circuits so that they develop the felt knowledge of riding a bike.

## The Influence of Our Group-Based Evolution as a Species

Some of these decisions we think are rational are not even our own. Anthropologists agree that we evolved in groups. We kept track of which members of our groups were good to work with whom. Today we would call them "reciprocal altruists." We also kept track of those who took advantage of us and did not pull their weight in the group. Today we would call them "free riders."

These traits got consolidated into our brains. Consider oxytocin, a neurochemical released by the pituitary gland when a mother nurses her baby. The tactile stimulation of the breast causes a neuroendocrine reflex that has the pituitary release oxytocin into the blood. This causes the smooth muscles in the breast to push the milk into its vestibule, where the baby can draw it out. It is a very nice example of a two-person reflex and why we are all here: We survived as a species because of nursing (at least evolutionarily, before the use of formula).

Given the usefulness of a bond between mother and baby, it is not surprising that oxytocin presents itself for this purpose. We must note that when we are talking about reflexes, this is an unconscious body response. Any nursing mother will agree: Lactating or ceasing to lactate on demand would be an excellent superpower while in public, especially when hearing the hungry baby of another recent mom cry. But that is not the case. Interestingly, men also possess the hormone oxytocin, and though they do not have the nursing reflex, it too seems to underlie emotional bonding. In a neuroeconomics game, where resources are exchanged, administering oxytocin causes people to be more generous with each other, even men. In fact, Paul Zak, a neuroeconomist, says a good way to release oxytocin in another person is to give them a welcome hug.[10]

How did we get here? The answer may be that when human societies were just forming early in our evolutionary history, it was advantageous to individuals to be in a group for reasons of labor division and defense. Evolution then selected biological mechanisms that promoted group work, with the oxytocin-releasing system being one of them. It does seem that our success as a human species is tied to our ability to work together in groups to accomplish goals. We find and support reciprocal altruists and punish or exclude free riders. To us, in looking at how college students make decisions, we see a big factor in group thinking, interaction with others, developing peer groups, having mentors, and so on. We also see the effects of social pressure in going along with the group and the society. Some of this sounds like system 1 from Kahneman. However, sometimes a group pressure outcome (maybe from FOMO, again) is unwisely rationalized by our deliberative cognitive systems in language. So, we say we believe something we know we should not. But that is another topic.

## Student Choice and the Impact on One College

Millennials wanted to find the jobs/careers that suited them, or so we were told.[11] Who doesn't? That may be one of the driving forces behind a remarkable story about Northeastern University where the applicant pool increased remarkably starting in about the year 2000, when millennials first hit their college years. Luckily for us, Jim was the dean of the College of Arts and Sciences at Northeastern starting in 1998 and had a front-row seat to this accomplishment. It illustrated how this experiential-based decision process is good for the higher education institution as well as the higher education student. Here is that story told by Jim:

> Before the ranking improvement accomplishment mentioned previously, Northeastern University had suffered an abrupt freshman enrollment decline. It had a large impact on the campus, and while that is a different story and not one we will tell here, the impact lingered. So, the institution was much more ready and willing to try something new in the aftermath. In Arts and Sciences, where Jim was the associate dean at the time, the idea was to develop a deeper embrace of the basic cooperative education principle for which the university was known. The idea began under Jim's predecessor, Robert Lowndes, and was carried forward when Jim followed him and became the dean.
>
> A group in the dean's office felt that the principles of experiential education, such as undergraduate research and study abroad, were already embedded in the culture of Arts and Sciences, but (with the exception of a few departments) the idea of cooperative education was not. In fact, there was a saying just before Jim and his colleagues took on this project that "cooperative education was no-op in Arts and Sciences." Some of them asked, "What could an English or history major do for a cooperative education internship?" Jim and his colleagues decided to see what would happen if they somehow really encouraged cooperative education experiences. Moreover, what if they could get the faculty governance of the college and the university to approve a change to

their graduation requirements, adding experiential education to math, writing, general education, and other degree areas? They did that in the year 2000.

There were two components to the requirement. The first was approximately 350 hours of direct experience, which the faculty of Arts and Sciences thought was easily met by doing one of the six-month, full-time cooperative education terms. They also stipulated that the requirement be met by the time spent in undergraduate research for ten hours per week over the course of two semesters, by studying abroad, by doing enough community service, or by other experiential activities students might propose. The second component was reflection, which is common across forms of experiential education. All of the then twenty-two College of Arts and Sciences departments had a senior capstone course with a very standard senior paper. Cooperative education or other experiences were welcome topics about which a student could write.

Although the faculty in Arts and Sciences was confident this cooperative education initiative would be a positive change, they were also concerned about how the students would adjust to it. The last thing they wanted was for the new requirement to potentially delay a student's graduation. So, the dean's office took the unusual step of appointing a faculty member in each department as an all-powerful "forgiveness angel" who could waive this college graduation requirement for any student.

But there was no need for them to have been worried. Only a handful of students needed forgiveness of the thousand or so who were graduating. What the faculty saw—though there was no control group here—was that students took the experiential requirement seriously, including cooperative education. Where the students at the other classical cooperative education colleges in the university (e.g., engineering or business) always took the cooperative education requirement seriously and planned for it from the beginning of their freshman year, the Arts and Sciences students started doing that with the new experiential education in all of its forms. It pays to have a requirement written down if one wants students to actually do it. It is also necessary that it works for them.

Jim and his colleagues did not expect what happened next. The College of Arts and Sciences exploded in admissions, SAT scores, and all those other metrics for success. The university began a marketing campaign at that time, and Jim was chosen to sit on the planning committee as a dean. In the budget crisis mentioned earlier, the trustees had set a limit on the freshman class size to enforce quality over quantity. Even so, Jim did not expect that over the next ten years that he was dean, the college's application pool would go from five thousand to fifteen thousand students (expanding from regional to national), the SAT scores would rise 250 points, and the number of students enrolled in the college would go from about three thousand to about six thousand.

As a result of this improvement in the College of Arts and Sciences and university-wide, the *US News & World Report* ranking of Northeastern University would go from about 165 to about 90 when Jim left the dean's office in 2008. The university ranking then continued to rise, getting close to 40. Northeastern had become one of the fastest-rising universities in American history. According to a recent article, in 2024, Northeastern University admitted only 5.2 percent of its applicant pool.[12] In an era of some colleges closing, Northeastern was bulletproof. In the school of Arts and Sciences, the faculty knew that their statistics made a major contribution to that rise. They felt the difference in student preparedness and saw it in their classes. One philosophy professor, who had told Jim early on that his job as dean was to make all of the students in his classes like his honors class that he had just taught, came to see Jim when he left the office and told Jim he did it. That was unusual.

Richard Freeland, the president of Northeastern from 1996 to 2006, wrote about this period of significant change in his book *Transforming the Urban University*.[13] For one thing, the tuition price rose as the admissions department selected not only the most talented students but also the ones who could most easily pay the tuition. It more than doubled, giving the university a much better financial picture than where it had been only a few years ago. The dean's office received inquiries about how they did it. They started a one-week summer camp for faculty and administrators at other universities called the Global Institute on Experiential Education.[14] It ran for about a dozen years, enrolling teams from approximately one hundred universities at the lovely Martha's Vineyard. The effect of having a national applicant pool did decrease the attendance rate of local Boston students—and with it the natural diversity of Northeastern's student body. The dean's office started some scholarship programs with admissions to try to encourage such students to attend, but when it came time for Jim to leave and eventually become a provost (the dean of the deans), he moved to the public sector, first at Queens College, CUNY and then at the University at Albany, SUNY. Those certainly were locations for a highly diverse student body.

The lessons we draw from this story for this book lie in the way the desires of students and their families shape what colleges do. This shaping occurs through the places where they apply and where they attend and whether they stay until they graduate. By showing up at this particular cooperative education university, they raised its profile. That leads us to our next point: We do know that what goes into making a university well known in a positive way is complicated, and indeed Northeastern worked on its reputation systematically so as to get far away from the budget crisis conditions mentioned before we told this story. In today's world, where it seems like every week we hear about a new college going out of business for enrollment reasons, this effect is important to the institution as well as to the individual student.

## A New Ranking Component on Upward Social: Economic Mobility

Universities and colleges love rankings, even when they hate them. In the past they were dependent on operational statistics such as entering freshman SAT scores, the graduation rates of the students, the number of PhDs, the extent of faculty scholarship, the funding resources of the institution, and its reputation for excellence among other senior administrators. These factors were always around, and together with some others they made up the general thinking as to which were the best colleges and universities. But in 1983, *US News & World Report* began publishing numeric rankings that attempted to make these evaluations more precise (or at least appear so). There was a lot of controversy when these rankings first came out. Nobody likes to be judged—especially when they do not win—and only a few predictable universities were at the top. We used these rankings in the previous story about Northeastern's rapid rise to make a point about a university making itself attractive to students by focusing not only on providing strong academics but also on helping the students succeed after college. Sometimes the right thing to do is also the most useful.

What is happening now is a bit different. The factors and ambitions of current students have not changed. What has changed is the data. It begins with a Harvard economist named Raj Chetty,[15] who used big data analytic techniques to analyze decades of US tax returns. He analyzed the difference between family income when a student started college and the student's income about ten years later, well after graduation. This had never been calculated before. What it showed was whether or not the college experience led to upward mobility. After all, a primary reason parents send their children to college is because they want them to do better economically than they did. Chetty's data showed which colleges were the best at helping students achieve that upward mobility, and as a result, that put pressure on colleges and universities to deliver.

The question of how colleges improve students' economic outcomes is a terribly important one, as many people today question the value of the time and money invested in higher education. We already mentioned the debt American college graduates carry, and while statistics show that a college degree still leads to more earning, what activities do those colleges provide that support this outcome? Without an answer to this question, higher education will continue to be vulnerable to competition from skill-based entities that may do a better job—and certainly a quicker and more affordable job—of getting students the skills they need to gain employment. But that would be a loss to everyone.

As many of us know, career paths are not linear. Students will need the breadth that a college education provides to be able to cope with change. Recently, AI produced a product called ChatGPT, and AI in general is making as much of a challenge to white-collar jobs as the invention of the automobile provided to horse-and-buggy manufacturers. Yet the economy survived that transition because people adapted. With the critical thinking training a college provides and the learning-to-learn that comes from both a broad and deep education that college also provides, we have our best chance of adapting. It is no wonder that the best jobs and the highest incomes still go to college graduates. A college of the future that combines its academic abilities with grounding in a chosen field will do well, as its reputation attracts enrollments, particularly if the price of tuition is not too high. We will come back to AI and the many benefits of good-fit personalized rankings to students, families, governments, and employers in later chapters. But we will not talk much here about how AI is currently reshaping teaching. That is for another book.

## Summary

Learning is of two minds. Or at least, it is going on in two parts of the student's mind: the cognitive and the emotional. There is the facts-and-theories mind, or what we said the late Daniel Kahneman called system 2. In cooking a meal or in a career, one needs to know the ingredients and how to put them together in the right order. But we all understand how cooking requires experience through practice so that the student can also learn at the gut level. Kahneman called this system 1. You are already built this way. It is what makes experiential education, on top of a fine academic curriculum, such a powerful combination. It turns out that this is good not only for the student but also for the institution. This brain-natural way of learning, integrating cognitive and emotional processes, is so important that it is the topic of the next chapter.

Chapter 3

# How the Brain Works to Divide Implicit and Explicit Thinking

Imagine you are a college student. You just left your physics lecture and are ready to dump all of that information from your brain because it is a Friday night. You have a fun weekend planned. You head back to your dorm room, effortlessly navigating across the quad and through the other students hustling to reach their next class on time, recognizing a few and giving a friendly head nod. Finally back in your room, it is time to decompress. Lucky for you, your roommates will not be back for an hour. You melt into the couch and zone out before the evening festivities begin.

For many college students, this sounds pretty typical. We've all been in that space where we want to shut off our mind and relax. But is it possible to shut off the mind? Answering that question completely risks us going down a philosophical and spiritual rabbit hole. But we do want to tell you a bit about daydreaming and how our brain has something called the "default mode network."

## Default Mode Neocortical Network in Humans

The concept of a default mode network in the brain was developed as scientists in the 1970s, particularly a Swedish scientist named David Ingvar, began to look at brain activity using the advancing technologies of brain scanners that measured regional cerebral blood flow.[1] These scanners could pinpoint the location where brain activity is happening at any particular moment because more activity in neural tissue means more blood flow. Brushing your teeth would show activity in one place, probably in the motor system, and then if we asked you to close your eyes and imagine your grandmother's face it would appear somewhere else, likely in the visual brain areas. Logic would say, then, that if you are not performing any task, be it physical or mental, the brain activity would be turned off. Of course, we don't mean in lower-level brain regions that control important body functions like breathing and the heartbeat. We mean in the more advanced processing areas of the brain.

Interestingly, though, what Ingvar found was that even if the mind is "at rest"—in other words, the subject is simply decompressing, daydreaming, or whatever you would like to call it—the brain is constantly active and working.[2] A few decades later, in the early 2000s, another scientist, this time from America, Marcus Raichle,[3] showed that the brain's energy consumption during a conscious task only increased about 5 percent from the baseline activity. This means that whether you're working on a complex physics problem or you're on the couch relaxing an hour later, the amount of activity that is going on in your brain is almost the same. As brain scanning techniques became more sophisticated, scientists were able to make increasingly detailed maps of this activity, representing a lack of conscious neural thought processes by the subject.

Has anyone ever asked you what you were thinking about and you click back to the present to respond with something along the lines of "Oh, nothing"? That is the feeling we're talking about here. To escape from that activity of thought is to enter what neuroscientists call the default mode network. This network is what constantly processes while you unconsciously continue to work on a problem despite lacking an active input or a conscious question at hand.

So what is the default mode network? To understand this question, one must understand the brain itself. While there are many neuroscientists working away to get down to the cellular and molecular level of how the brain works, we just want you to know that the brain is like a map. In relatively the same region in all of our brains, we have stored our memory of how to pour a bowl of cereal in the morning. When we taste the cereal in our mouth, the same brain region will be active. If we twist the cap back onto the milk using our right hand, indeed again, we will see activity in the same region for each of us. Interestingly, a monkey doing the same task would have a similar pattern in a similar region. As humans, though, we have extremely advanced brains, and these regions that perform basic functions can communicate with one another through the cells we call neurons. This gives us the ability to create vast groupings of interconnected regions that we refer to as "networks."

The default mode network is a large web of brain regions composed of these neurons, beginning in the front of the brain: the frontal cortex. The frontal lobe, which is involved in logic and planning, contains neurons that extend to a junction of multiple other lobes of the brain that are involved in vision, sound, and spatial perception. This is called the temporo-parietal-occipital junction, and it can be found a little bit above and behind the ear on both sides of the head. We have a good understanding of what all of these brain regions do separately, but a functional relationship between them is far less understood. The interesting thing to us, though, is that when someone is tasked with a goal-directed action or a highly cognitive, thought-evoking behavior like kicking a soccer ball or completing a math problem, this web of brain networks shuts off. To turn this network on, what do you have to do? Brain scans reveal the answer is quite simple: Think about nothing.[4] Neuroscientists and others tend to call this "implicit thinking," or the stream of thoughts occurring often outside of conscious awareness. This is in comparison with "explicit thinking," which is task-oriented.

## A Closer Look at the Frontal Cortex and Implicit Thinking Network

Zooming in on the front of the brain during implicit thinking specifically, we see two major regions of activity. The first is a bit higher up toward the top of your head and is called the dorsomedial prefrontal cortex. While its name is less important, it is significant that research has strongly implicated this area in empathy and responsiveness to social interactions.[5] Meanwhile, the ventromedial prefrontal cortex, which is located nearby but a bit lower in the brain, just above your nose, is involved in reward-based decision-making behavior.[6]

This value hub in the brain has been studied in neuroeconomics,[7] a field whose name was coined by neuroscientist Paul Glimcher in the 1990s and that focuses on the computational and psychological processes of choice. In his classic example, he uses a brain scanner to show the activity of subjects making choices involving monetary rewards. More specifically, the research team asked participants to choose between a smaller, guaranteed monetary reward and a larger reward with some level of uncertainty. As expected, the prefrontal cortex was highly active when the subject was faced with a more risky option. A 50 percent chance at a one-hundred-dollar reward or a 90 percent chance at a ten-dollar reward: Which would you choose? We see our college students weighing this option all the time as they research which courses to get an "easy A" with minimal effort or else a B with a huge amount of work but a stronger educational foundation for subsequent courses.

One interesting thing about this region is that it contains a special type of neuron called a von Economo neuron.[8] These neurons were identified almost a century ago and have a unique shape and function, being long and spindly with connections that travel far distances through multiple layers of the human cortex. Given the way these neurons span several brain areas, they have received much attention for having a role in consciousness.[9] Because of their presence in regions of the prefrontal cortex and default mode network, we believe that these neurons could be involved in implicit thinking and communication with our lower, much more evolutionarily conserved emotional system of the brain called the limbic system. After all, if there is activity in this default mode network when the brain is at rest, there has to be some kind of unconscious communication happening. With the potentially active von Economo neurons located in the areas of social cognition, emotion, and motivation, perhaps rather than just feeding our behavior and focus on a task, these neurons are communicating deeper into the brain and modifying implicit circuits that we can't necessarily put a finger on but can feel driving our simple decisions such as "I like this class" or "This subject just isn't for me."

## The Deeper Limbic System of the Brain

Our limbic system is yet another complex network of brain structures, but this one plays a central role in the regulation of a range of emotions and motivated behaviors. The primary function of the limbic system is processing and regulating emotions at the implicit or unconscious level. Our primary feelings like fear, anger, and happiness all stem from structures within the limbic system. It is also critical for memory as well as motivation—specifically, our reward pathway, which includes a concentration of neurons that use the neurotransmitter dopamine. These neurons play a huge role in pleasure, impulse, and reinforcement learning. In a laboratory, that might be a rat pressing a bar to receive an injection of cocaine. That reward effect comes straight from the dopamine reward circuit in our limbic system. A student staying up late to put those final touches on an essay so they can earn the A? That falls in the same circuit. Today, even the word "dopamine" is used to talk about things we find attractive, like playing video games.

The limbic system does not work in isolation; it interacts with many brain regions to perform its complex functions. Additionally, it is highly interconnected with the neocortex, which includes connectivity to regions in our prefrontal cortex shared by the default mode network (which is, again, also implicitly thinking). In fact, we believe that the cortex, which is responsible for higher-level functions like cognition and decision-making, encodes or integrates information from the limbic system, which again is primarily involved in emotion, memory, and motivation. This mapping or encoding of information from the limbic system to the cortex has more recently been referred to as "re-representation." And it is critical to form more highly evolved cognitive functions that operate on value as well as logic.

For example, our college students are often heavily swayed by emotional decisions rather than rational ones (and so is everyone). During academic advising, we coauthors are both accustomed to students entering our offices with a carefully mapped out plan for the next semester, oftentimes involving a complete background check on each professor by asking friends for their opinions and checking things out on ratemyprofessors.com. Through this process, the student gains an understanding of what they are getting themselves into, encoded implicitly into their thoughts, planning, and judgment. As we said earlier, this emotional information from the limbic system is then symbolically re-represented in the cortex and subject to an explicit review by our more advanced cortical structures. Questions then arise, such as "Do I take the harder course with an excellent professor to gain a better understanding, but potentially earn a poor grade?" and "Do I take the easy way out with the far less challenging professor who only gives take-home exams?"

While we will delve further into this in chapter 10, citing specific brain regions and interconnectivity, right now it is important just to understand we have a mental map. We have connectivity from the deeper, emotional implicit brain and the higher, more sophisticated and analytical explicit brain. And these regions communicate. The ultimate decision that is made is a result of combining our inner limbic information with our more sophisticated cortex for evaluation and analysis. This is constantly happening in active thought, but it is being reanalyzed and reprocessed as the default mode network keeps this information exchange going.

Antonio Damasio refers to this communication, and maybe the von Economo neurons themselves, as the "convergence-divergence network" underlying consciousness.[10] Damasio believes that consciousness arises from the integration of sensory, emotional, and bodily information, and says so in his book *Descartes' Error*.[11] The integration of neural signals from brain regions of all levels is designed to process sensory input, emotional responses, and internal physiological states of the body. The convergence of this information results in information moving from areas of implicit meaning to areas of explicit thought. Emotions, stemming from the limbic system, manifest as implicit processes that weigh on explicit thoughts. When making decisions, individuals implicitly consider the emotional consequences associated with different choices. This involves the convergence of information from emotional brain regions with the cognitive processes of the higher-level cortex.

Bringing this back to the default mode network is evidence that your brain is constantly sending information between different regions—despite your perception that you are thinking about nothing. This information travels through areas known to be associated with explicit thinking and consciousness all the way down to regions implicated in implicit thinking and the unconscious processing of decisions. These regions talk. They have to talk because if they did not, our college students would not be able to make the choice of "I like this major because I find history extremely fascinating" or "I hate this major because I can't even bring myself to read this boring history book." Von Economo neurons, with their huge branches traveling long distances through the brain, could be a critical piece for this communication.

## The Great Divide Between Processing in the Limbic System and the Cortex

When students have experiences like internships at a workplace, and especially when the implicit parts of that experience impact their conscious plans for a field of study, we think this is likely when the default mode network is active and explicit-implicit thinking happens. But prompting explicit-implicit thinking is not as easy as one would expect. Students certainly know what happened in terms of their feelings. One student interning in a law firm hates it and tells us that lawyers are all trying to one-up each other and that the law is about as exciting as reading the dictionary. Another student tells us that lawyers are like priests translating the written law into social justice and the law itself is like the Rosetta Stone of our aspirations for fairness. They praise the order that is brought out by the lawyers and judges from the real world of messy arrangements, such as apartment leases that could become the subject of a lawsuit to get what we used to call "slum landlords" to fix up their apartments. After that experience, it is quite easy to guess which student is likely to continue their college studies and go to law school and who will be changing their major the following semester. This becomes a problem, though, when the student puts off that hands-on learning until late in their undergraduate career or, even worse, following their graduation.

The small exercise just mentioned is actually rich with how reflection (consciously, explicitly) upon the reaction to an experience (emotionally, implicitly) improves student learning with experiential education. We will return to how this works and the challenge of turning implicit reactions into explicit plans that can be explained, especially as in the case of a mother who always thought their child would be a lawyer. While this kind of confirmation leads to passion, which leads to deeper study, which leads to success, what we want to focus on here in this chapter and book is the way the student who had this experience now seems more mature. They can better integrate what they are learning in academic classes with what they see as their ultimate profession, whether it be further schooling or, most commonly, securing a job after graduation. This is most definitely detectable by employers and admission committees. Of course, they want the more mature student and one who is focused on their job or field of further study. They want professional wisdom. So do the students.

To get there, we have to bridge this explicit-implicit thinking divide, which seems to be a characteristic of how our brain works and why students sometimes find themselves surprised by the thoughts and feelings that pop into their minds from seemingly random places. To understand how to create this bridge between implicit and explicit learning, we must understand how the brain learns and how information is transferred from learning to habit. We must understand how the conscious, active mind connects with implicit, unconscious processes. In a way, it is the exact reverse of how implicit circuits and emotion influence our explicit decision-making. As neuroscientists, of course we are interested in this, but colleges and universities should also be interested. They should teach students to access this communication of complex networks and long-spanning neuron connections because its integration enables the professional wisdom that employers are constantly looking to find.

## Summary

The concept of the default mode network in the human brain was developed in the 1970s as scientists like David Ingvar used advanced brain scanning technology to study brain activity. They discovered that even when the brain is at rest—not focused on any specific task—it remains constantly active. The default mode network is a web of interconnected brain regions, primarily involving the frontal cortex, temporo-parietal-occipital junction, and prefrontal cortex. It becomes active when the brain is not engaged in goal-directed tasks, facilitating what is known as implicit thinking—thoughts occurring outside of conscious awareness. This contrasts with explicit thinking, which involves conscious, task-oriented thought processes. It also interacts closely with the limbic system, a network responsible for regulating emotions and motivated behaviors. This interaction enables the integration of emotional and cognitive processes, referred to as re-representation, where emotional information from the limbic system is mapped onto the cortex for higher-level evaluation and decision-making. This process is crucial for forming complex cognitive functions and making informed decisions. Understanding the default mode network and interaction with the limbic system could help explain how implicit and explicit thinking processes are connected, influencing our decisions and behaviors. This knowledge can be valuable for educational institutions in teaching students to harness this communication between complex networks to develop professional wisdom and informed decision-making skills, which we will discuss further in the following chapters.

Chapter 4

# A Deeper Look at Implicit Brain Processes and Neuroplasticity

We mentioned already that our understanding of the brain has evolved significantly over the past few centuries, indeed over the last few decades. As neuroscience researchers, we believe that this understanding extends beyond single neurons in the brain, creating unimaginably intertangled networks that are slowly being figured out. To understand this, and to understand wise men before us such as Blaise Pascal when he stated that "the heart has its reasons, which reason knows nothing of," we must briefly look at the evolution of neuroscience, understand the concept of neuroplasticity, and not lose the idea that professional knowledge is developed through a delicate explicit-implicit interplay that is shaped by our head and our metaphorical heart.

## Hundreds of Years of an Evolving Brain Understanding

In ancient times, the brain was often misunderstood or overlooked in favor of other organs. For example, in ancient Egypt, the heart was considered the center of intelligence and emotions. Greek philosophers like Hippocrates and Aristotle made attempts to understand the brain's functions, but their ideas were often speculative and lacked empirical evidence. It wasn't until the Renaissance and Enlightenment that early anatomists began to study the brain itself as an important control center in the body. Descartes was the first to propose that the pineal gland, a tiny region smack-dab in the center of the human cerebral cortex, was the seat of the soul.[1] While we now know that this region is a hub for releasing melatonin and governing the body's sleep-wake cycle, it is important to note that until this point, the brain was barely given any credit for its complex functions in governing the human body.

Fast-forwarding over the neuroscientific advancements of the nineteenth and twentieth centuries, neuroscientists have been able to disprove many theories, such as the one that human traits could be determined by the shape of the skull. Made popular by Franz Joseph Gall, this practice was called phrenology.[2] Imagine going into your guidance counselor's office as a high school student, and rather than taking an aptitude test to help guide you to your strengths and potential interests in college, your guidance counselor stood behind you, rolled up their sleeves, and started rubbing their fingers all across your head for clues about your intelligence, strengths, and weaknesses.

We have also been able to identify not only interconnected circuits but specific neurons that encode various memories, functions, and behaviors in the brain. Modern science has given us ways to measure the electrical conductivity in the brain through electroencephalography (EEG) at the skull surface. This has led to the association of brain wave patterns with some different mental states. To go inside the brain, a surgeon could implant electrodes in an epilepsy patient to record such activity at depth, but we have a better way: using functional magnetic resonance imaging (fMRI), positron emission tomography (PET), and other methods to scan brain activity at greater depth, without any invasive surgeries. Brain scanners are revolutionizing human neuroscience as we attempt to understand neural connectivity during thoughts and behaviors. We have discovered neurotransmitters, single tiny molecules that act like locks and keys in the brain to influence our behavior by activating and deactivating pieces of circuits. Much work is being done on the genetics of the brain, and very clear links have been identified between different behavioral conditions and predispositions. In less complex animals like a worm and recently a fruit fly, neuroscientists are mapping every neuron and all of its connections in a field called connectomics. With the current neuroimaging, molecular biology, and genetic components, there is a lot of potential to unlock still unknown mechanisms of the brain.

As scientists continue to move closer to pinpointing and understanding the precise mechanisms of structure and function, they must keep in mind that this stagnant image of one moment in time does not truly encompass what's happening as the brain is dynamic, living, and changing every fraction of a second. In the brain of the freshman college student that was set on being a crime scene investigator because of one too many episodes of *Criminal Minds*, *Law & Order*, or *CSI*, there are great capacities, and these capacities include the ability to change. The brain is adaptable, something that we like to call neuroplastic. Those neurons, that advanced wiring we have connecting networks of implicit and explicit thought, are not rigid. That excitement that our student feels each time they hear a siren or step into their forensic chemistry lab is only a snapshot. It can fade or be abruptly stopped with one small hiccup in the road, one failed exam because of an absence or inability to study, one teacher with whom the student does not jive well, or one experience, such as not being able to solve that first huge case, that changes that feeling forever. It causes the brain to rewire. Driven by experience, we are constantly changing our neural networks, giving us the ability to, as we like to believe, develop that thing we call professional wisdom.

## Learning to Like What You Like: Neuroplasticity at an Implicit Level

One of our most basic, evolutionarily conserved brain circuits that we share with even our animal counterparts is called the "dopamine reward circuit," or the mesolimbic reward pathway of the brain. You've probably heard of dopamine as that "feel-good" neurotransmitter that is released when you score an A on an exam or take a big bite of your favorite chocolate cake that your mother only makes once a year.

Dopamine is a driver for behavior. It works in our implicit brain to motivate decision-making without our explicit processing. This is why our cats also feel good when they hear that sound of their automatic feeder going off or you can see that look of happiness in your dog's face when you get home from a long day of work.

As we mentioned, the Princeton psychologist Daniel Kahneman won the Nobel Prize in Economics in 2002 and later published a book in 2011 called *Thinking, Fast and Slow*[3] that focuses on two modes of thinking. Kahneman describes "thinking fast" as an automatic and intuitive mode of thinking, or implicit. It operates effortlessly and quickly but sometimes can lead us to cognitive biases and errors. "Thinking slow," on the other hand, is unhurried, deliberative, and analytical. It requires more cognitive effort and is often used for complex problem-solving and decision-making.

Shifting this to the lens of a neuroscientist, what Kahneman is likely talking about with thinking fast is an implicit brain circuit—a fast-thinking, dopamine-driven, impulsive one that shouts, "I want this now!" Sometimes this circuit dominates in behaviors that are not necessarily the best choice for the human at that moment, such as a college student staying all night at a party when they have an exam they should be studying for or, in a more extreme case, an addict seeking out a drug despite all economic and personal costs. Thinking slow, though, involves more careful consideration of long-term consequences and a more explicit lens of thought. This thought is much less of a shout but rather a rational logic: "I should not do this because it's not my best idea and I'm going to be in trouble with the school or my parents." To understand the role of the mesolimbic reward pathway in this, we must first understand what dopamine is really doing in the brain; and to talk about dopamine, we must talk about a father of dopamine work, Wolfram Schultz.

Schultz's work on dopamine began in the 1990s, when he studied the activity of dopamine neurons in the brains of primates involved in reward-based tasks. Again, dopamine is released when something good happens. Maybe you found a twenty-dollar bill on the ground or took a bite of a fantastic sandwich. Schultz took this a step further and discovered that these dopamine neurons become active when an *unexpected* reward was received, giving an entirely new level of complexity to this "reward" or "feel-good" neurotransmitter. Over time, he found that the activity of the neurons would actually shift from responding to the reward itself to predicting when a reward would occur.[4] For that college student, when the professor hands back that weekly quiz that you scored an A on, dopamine is released. A few weeks into the class, though, the stimulus becomes conditioned and, interestingly, dopamine is no longer released in response to receiving that piece of paper back with a bold, red A marked on the top of it. Instead, the brain actually releases the flood of that feel-good neurotransmitter to the sight of the professor in the front of the room with that stack of graded quizzes.

Thus, the capacities of dopamine in the brain seem to be more of a monitor of reward and expectation rather than the black-and-white "pleasure" transmitter as which it is often referred to. With this ability, dopamine plays a huge role in facilitating behavior in response to experience. Imagine you're at the first day of your summer internship as a legal aid at your county law office. You were selected out of dozens of applicants for this position and know that this experience will really help your application to law school when you start applying in the fall. You've done your research on the office and you keep hearing one thing: Avoid the county executive at all costs. Rumor has it he terminated the last intern that was in your exact position during the first week of the internship as well as numerous other junior members of the team over the past year. At the office-wide meeting later that day, you intentionally sit in the back of the crowded room, as you are already overwhelmed with your first-day jitters and you know that you do not want to meet eyes with anyone, especially the county executive.

As soon as the meeting begins, you see that the first thing on the agenda is an introduction of new staff. You get a feeling of discomfort deep in your stomach as you think about the possibility of forgetting your own name or where you go to school in the room of all your new coworkers. Worse than that, you see the county executive sitting right in the front of the room with a look on his face that clearly says how much he does not want to be in that meeting. No pressure. Luckily, your moment comes and goes quickly, and you blur into the other five new hire introductions. Your nerves calm by the end of the meeting.

As you're getting up to leave, though, you see the county executive heading straight for you in a beeline that you simply cannot maneuver away from. You see him raise his hand in a gesture and he asks you to hold up a minute, addressing you by name specifically. You start running through every possible outcome in your mind. Did you say something wrong? Are you being terminated on the first day? Should you not have sat in the back of the room? Is it too late to just quit? What could he possibly want to talk to a first-day intern about? Why not the other hires?

Expecting the worst, that's not what happens at all. It turns out that you and the county executive's son attend the same college, and he wanted to ask you about your experience there. You chat for a good twenty minutes, and at the end of the conversation, he gives you his personal cell phone number in case any issues arise during your internship. Not only that, he follows up with you a few days later in an email to make sure that you're enjoying your position. Every time you see him in the hallway, he warmly says hello, and a few times he even stops at your cubicle to check and see if you need anything. By the end of the summer, he knows your list of dream law schools just as well as you do and has already offered to write a letter of recommendation for you. You think back to those rumors you heard about him and wonder where they came from, because this person was not what you expected. He had become your mentor and clearly wanted to see you succeed.

Going into this situation with a negative expectation meant a few things. First off, when you saw the county executive, your behavior and explicit thought would be to avoid him at all costs. No dopamine release here, as the emotion evoked was more so one of fear and anxiety. After that first interaction, though, your brain began to implicitly rewire. Not only did it begin to see the county executive in a positive light, but by the end of the summer, even just the sound of his voice down the hall speaking with another employee made you feel a sense of relaxation and a hint of excitement for a chance to catch up with him if he was heading in your direction.

The dopamine patterns of your implicit circuits were not only formed in this case but actually shifted to stimuli associated with your new mentor rather than just the conversations with him. This dopamine release could even be elicited by something as simple as seeing another tall, brown-haired businessman in a blue suit with a blue tie (the same thing you always saw the county executive wearing daily). This is because our implicit dopamine circuits have the ability to grow and change, and this can heavily influence our explicit thoughts and actions. The same thing happens when a premed student enters that dreaded organic chemistry class on the first day, wondering if there is even a chance that they make it through not one but two long semesters. But add a teacher that is engaging, personable, and fun to the equation, and the students can not only learn organic chemistry itself but also learn to actually like organic chemistry.

## Changing What You Like: Neuroplasticity at an Implicit Level

Another thing about these dopamine neurons is that they are intelligent, with an ability to signal the difference between the predicted reward and the actual reward. When an outcome is better than expected, dopamine neurons actually increase their firing rate to create a positive prediction error. Conversely, when an outcome is worse than expected, dopamine neurons decrease their firing rate, resulting in a negative prediction error. This is a fundamental process to learning and decision-making, all relying on this single neurotransmitter and all happening in our implicit processes. If you went into that quiz expecting to earn a C but you actually earned an A, it causes an even higher release of dopamine in the brain. The opposite is true if you were to receive an F when expecting a C. Thus, in simple terms, the more unexpected a reward, the higher the amount of the pleasure transmitter that is released. Your brain knows the difference between "seriously awesome" and just plain old "good" and allows you to feel this.

This phenomenon is a huge driver of our implicit learning. I'm sure you've heard the phrase "practice makes perfect," but is that really the case? In a study by Miglioretti et al. over a decade ago, it was shown that in trained radiologists—that is, those who completed four years of college, four years of medical school, and a five-year residency program with an optional two-year fellowship after that—their ability to diagnose a patient does not get better with age.[5] This is counterintuitive, right? When you think of the wisest doctor, the one that you're going to trust with your life, you're probably not going to pick the bright-eyed thirty-two-year-old that's rounding on their second week as an attending in the hospital. Rather, it makes sense to go with the experienced doctor with gray hair, glasses, and leadership awards and accolades that accompany thirty years of experience under their belt. It would only make sense that over all of this time in the field, they would develop into a better clinician.

The interesting thing, though, is that this trend depends on the area of medicine, and we believe this is because of our implicit dopamine learning circuits. The secret to improving a skill is to have explicit control over it while practicing. During the many years of medical training, from watching a first surgery or making a first diagnosis, the thought process is explicit. As you begin to master your diagnostic or technical craft, this learning changes to an implicit process, and this affords our doctors the ability to learn more or improve and refine their skills. The more that is mastered, the more we can improve, and improvement comes with learning. Learning is an immediate process of our intrinsic dopamine neurons. Remember that positive and negative prediction error? Well, that is going to be a huge component of this process.

Now let's look at what's happening with our radiologists. Radiology is a field of medicine that involves diagnosing injuries and diseases by looking at medical images. Radiologists are often consulted by other types of doctors, such as oncologists, orthopedic surgeons, or neurosurgeons, to aid in the interpretation of a case. For many radiologists, practicing does not have to be deliberate. Rather, radiologists interpret images, send them back to the primary provider who is treating the patient, and with that they are done with the case. If there isn't a second round of imaging or consultation, that radiologist will likely not hear the treatment or outcome for that patient.

Let's say that a neurologist was the one who ordered that patient's brain scan, and the radiologist missed the presence of a tumor in the somatosensory cortex that was causing tingling and numbness in the patient's right hand. At this point the neurosurgeon would shift their diagnoses and begin investigating other potential causes outside of the brain, such as spinal cord or nerve damage. It would likely take months before the patient's brain was rescanned, giving the radiologist any insight that they indeed missed the tumor. At that point, it is highly unlikely they even remember the case, and within the dopamine circuits that underlie our implicit learning, there would be no prediction error at all. Because they're not grooming those implicit circuits, we believe that's why radiologists don't improve over time with their diagnostic ability.

Let's look at the surgeon in the next room over working on a different patient having a tumor removed. Surgery is vastly different from radiology in that the patient outcome is immediate. A positive outcome, or successful surgery, would affect our dopamine circuits. Moreover, a successful surgery when the probability of success was extremely low would cause an even greater dopamine release, or positive prediction error, whereas the opposite is also true. If a surgery were to be unsuccessful and the patient did not make it through the procedure despite a high chance of success, this would result in a negative prediction error and drastic decrease in the firing of our dopamine in neurons in the implicit circuitry. From this, our surgeons learn. Numerous studies have shown this is indeed the case, with the peak age for a surgeon being between forty-five and fifty years old (remembering that the aging body does put physical limitations on a surgeon's skill).[6]

So, while our radiologist isn't getting any more accurate over the years, our surgeon is doing exactly the opposite. With every surgery, they are becoming more skilled at their craft. This is because they are constantly receiving feedback on their performance, and dopamine neurons thrive on this feedback. Dopamine neurons modify their communication with and influence on the body's behavior and perception—all of that explicit thought and action—based on the feedback they're receiving. The question of whether or not someone "likes" an internship, a field of study, or a class is all based on the experiences that they've had previously and the immediate outcomes of those experiences. Without those experiences, we have a cap for knowledge and skill. We are that radiologist. While we might be excellent, our circuits aren't challenged to improve or to learn. Without those experiences, we can't truly unlock our professional wisdom.

## The Neuroplastic Brain and the Plasticity of Higher Education

As academic advisors to many students on the premed track, we often hear from medical schools that we are providing them students who can memorize facts, but that's where things stop. This is a great tool, of course, to pass the MCAT (the standardized test for medical school entry) and the Step 1 boards exam that comes halfway through the medical school experience. These tests are solely focused on "What did you learn?" After these exams, though, students switch their testing to clinical competency exams and are required to pass Step 2, which has a large focus on clinical knowledge. In addition to that, they must receive excellent letters of recommendation from clinical faculty to be competitive for a residency position. No longer is the focus on memorization—it is about skills. So how can we train this earlier in one's career so that they are capable of making this shift?

A liberal arts education is a first step toward this. In these programs, students develop their critical thinking skills, communication, and creativity that advance the student beyond a memorization robot, as we like to say. Offering and taking more courses in cultural competency, social determinants of health, and health care ethics also help our students to see through that bigger, explicit lens earlier in their health care careers. Medical schools are now requiring clinical hours prior to acceptance. We are seeing more and more high school students seeking out applied learning experiences, such as shadowing, even before matriculating to colleges.

Colleges are great—some more than others—at developing this implicit knowledge. It is the explicit that traditionally comes from outside of the classroom. Both are important, but both are not developed and nurtured at the same rate in our current educational systems. We want to set our graduates up to be either the radiologists or the surgeons, depending on the passions they develop throughout their experiences in their medical school journey. We are still learning the best way to do this, though, and education is still shifting as we get closer to our target. Just like the brain with its neuroplasticity and ability to change in response to stimuli, our education system can do this as well. We will talk about this more in future chapters, but for now, we must discuss exactly how this implicit-explicit information transfer is happening and exactly how that is manifesting in our behavior.

All of this applies to the development of professional wisdom, as we will discuss in chapter 6. The secret we will see is learning from the experience, getting the feedback from your actions, and applying that to the knowledge you carry. Indeed, it is the interaction of that explicit knowledge (thinking slow) with the implicit knowledge (thinking fast) that gives you the "feel" for what you are doing as well as the knowledge about it. This is projected to others, like the hiring manager, at an implicit or gut level, and it appears in you as a situational confidence. That is the beginning of professional wisdom.

## Summary

The understanding of the brain has evolved over centuries. Modern neuroscience has identified interconnected circuits and specific neurons responsible for various functions and behaviors. Techniques like EEG, MRI, and PET scans (along with the discovery of neurotransmitters) have deepened our understanding of brain activity and its genetic links to behavior. Dopamine, a key neurotransmitter, plays a crucial role in the brain's reward system, influencing decision-making and behavior. Psychologist Daniel Kahneman's concepts of thinking fast and thinking slow parallel neuroscientific ideas of implicit, dopamine-driven decision-making and explicit, deliberative thought. In education, fostering both implicit and explicit knowledge is crucial. Liberal arts education, courses in cultural competency, and practical experiences like shadowing can help students develop critical thinking and clinical skills. As educational systems evolve, they can better prepare students for professional challenges by integrating both types of knowledge. Ultimately, professional wisdom arises from the interplay of explicit knowledge and implicit, experience-based learning. This blend of understanding and intuition projects confidence and competence, which is crucial for professional success.

## Chapter 5

# Crossing the Implicit-Explicit Threshold While Moving from Learning to Habit

Internships are extremely variable depending on your specialty area. After all, it's highly unlikely that you want a college sophomore who is interning for the summer at your local hospital to be the one setting your broken bone after that incident you had on your bicycle. Let's save that for the orthopedist. On the other hand, it's extremely likely that the student interning at a machinist's shop over the summer would be hands-on with the equipment, doing everything from producing that intended part to troubleshooting that machine that makes the strange grinding noise. They may even go a step further to really impress their supervisor by creating their own technical drawing for an innovative solution to a pesky problem. If they are lucky, maybe the supervisor would even put the welding torch in the student's hand and give them the supplies to build that newfangled anchor to fix that problem themselves.

Which one of these is more important for our college students? Should academic advisors be pushing students toward a hands-on experience, or is it just as valuable to watch and learn? Not surprisingly, different brain regions underlie the formation of new memories, like how to identify a Pott's fracture versus a calcaneal fracture (both foot bones) on an x-ray of the ankle, and the formation of new motor skills, like how to accurately bend that piece of steel with ease at the perfect temperature. Learning is only one part of this equation, too—the explicit part. Soon enough that information is transferred from those active learning circuits to the habit or implicit circuit, where recognizing that image or performing that movement can actually occur without conscious thought. That might sound a little crazy, but we've all walked and talked, not thinking about the patterned movement of our feet keeping us moving forward. Those implicit circuits and learned brain activity patterns allow us to do this. Thus, the more information our brain is able to move from active learning to habit, the better we can thrive in that internship as we can concentrate on what is coming up next.

If you are looking for the best surgeon to perform a surgery on your loved one, you likely want the doctor that has an impressive resume. With that, you want your doctor to not only have come out at the top of their medical school class but to also have attended an excellent residency program and fellowship training for many more years of hands-on experience. Also having a huge number of successful cases with the exact procedure that you are looking for them to perform is important too. When employers look at applicants, they look for the same things. And not all college degrees are created equal. A degree from Harvard University would likely hold more weight than a degree from your local community college. It is the same with experience. An internship at Google would be more impressive than an internship at your uncle's computer repair shop. The question is how we in higher education build the best applicant for an employer who wants both the book smarts and the physical skills.

## Multiple Types of Learning Exist

Let's start with Ivan Pavlov, who showed that dogs would learn to salivate to a bell by simply repeatedly ringing that bell just before giving the dog the food. Dogs always reflexively salivate to food, but now these dogs would salivate if Pavlov rang the bell. In psychology that is called classical conditioning, and it works on reflexes like salivation or eyeblink. B. F. Skinner added to the field of learning by showing conditioning of voluntary behaviors. Here, a hungry rat might be trained to press a lever on the wall of a chamber that produces a reward like food. Once the animal does it perhaps several times, it figures out that behavior leads to the reward. We all know that if you want to train your dog to sit, offer it a treat after it performs that behavior. If you want your dog not to do something, like go to the bathroom in the house, give it a punishment (such as a loud scolding) whenever it misbehaves, and the behavior is less likely to happen again. It works the same way when you reward a student with an A for completing an assignment. This is called operant conditioning.

Looking closer at classical conditioning, humans have a brain region called the amygdala that has earned a reputation as the fear center of the brain. Classical conditioning would argue that earning an F on that paper soon enough would cause you to not only have a negative reaction to the grade but to also have a negative emotional response to the professor. That is the dopamine shift we talked about before with Schultz. What we know about the amygdala is that it receives input from the somatosensory brain regions and outputs to multiple body circuits, including the centers that impact things such as breathing rate and heart rate. So, this integration center has the ability to not only govern behavior, but learning occurs when that sensory information coming in is actually paired with a previously neutral stimulus. This is done through synaptic plasticity, or the ability of the brain's cells to rewire with repeated exposure to specific stimuli. In the case of the student earning an F, the original aversive stimuli (that bad grade) soon links itself together through changes in the connectivity within the amygdala and its subregions. So now every time the student sees that professor, they get that same feeling in the pit of their gut, their heart rate increases, they start to sweat, and they want to turn in the opposite direction.

Looking at the flip side, though, the same thing happens when neurons in the brain form new connections in an area of the brain associated with reward called the nucleus accumbens. The reason that you happen to like a professor that continually gives you that A you worked hard to earn, even on the days they are not giving back an assignment, is because of this classical conditioning. In theory, if we were somehow able to give you a shot of a drug that changed your body's homeostasis (or baseline) to a negative state, similarly to what experimenters do with animals when placing a bad-tasting substance such as quinine in their mouth, we could potentially overcome that nucleus accumbens reward/feel-good response and condition it away with the aversive stimuli. Our point again is that the brain is plastic and these circuits can modify themselves based on the incorporation of additional variables.

Operant conditioning, on the other hand, that other form of stimulus-response learning, is important as a key for learning from your environment. This type of learning is voluntary and active, unlike classical conditioning. Rather than associating a neutral stimulus to a meaningful reflexive response (the way our student associated their professor and/or the course with that gut-wrenching anguish after an F and developed a reflexive negative reaction), here a neutral stimulus is paired with a reward or a punishment that will draw out or suppress a voluntary action. This way, behaviors are strengthened or weakened based on their outcome. Every student that's been reprimanded by their parents, grounded, or had their cell phone taken away for a specific amount of time is familiar with the tactic of operant conditioning. Teachers for students of all ages, and even some of your college professors, have seen this firsthand, in that even college students get excited for stickers on their exams that are only given out when they get an A. Even many semesters later, students come back saying, "I remember that's the only quiz I got a sticker on!," which shows the huge impact of this tiny reward on their learning and memory. If only all of the material from that exam was as easy for students to recall.

For learning to take place in the form of operant conditioning, several brain regions are involved. First, there has to be communication between the sensory information coming into the brain for processing and the motor areas that control the behavioral going out that we physically see. There are two major pathways between these areas. One is a direct cerebral connection (we call this transcortical, as it goes between areas of the neocortex). The second connection is through an older region called the basal ganglia that lies beneath the neocortex. The transcortical connections are important for coding the series of events in an activity. Push the bar, get the reward. As a human, you know that learning is much more complex than this, but we can tell you how to change the oil on your car's engine step-by-step. Does that mean you should do it? Well, probably not if it's your first try. Could you, though? Yes, because of these transcortical connections linking what's coming in (sensory, like sound) to what's going out (motor, like moving your hands to slide over the hood release lever and open the hood). As these behaviors continue to be repeated, they move from predominantly transcortical to moving through the basal ganglia pathway. We associate this with a shift from active learning to habit, which we will talk about a bit more in the next section.

Regarding our hungry rat pushing a lever for a food pellet, operant conditioning would suggest that the initial behavior of bar pressing—which only weakly activated neurons in the brain at the early sight of the bar in combination with whatever reason (perhaps just curiosity) that caused the rat to press the lever for the first time—plus that unexpected reward causes a change in the brain. In this context, the basal ganglia plays a crucial role, as it helps in the formation and execution of goal-directed behaviors. The basal ganglia acts as a hub between the neural pathways of reinforcement (which we discussed in the previous chapter) that were controlled by dopamine and the physical execution of the motor behavior. With every repeated press of that lever, those neurons that previously were not rapidly firing begin to form a stronger connection, learning that pressing the lever will deliver that food pellet the hungry rat's reward center desires as a tasty treat. Again, learning is only possible because our existing neurons are neuroplastic and have the ability to change by strengthening the connections of neurons that are in close communication. This is where the famous phrase from neuropsychologist Donald Hebb originated: "Neurons that fire together, wire together."[1]

In addition to stimulus-response learning, the brain also performs perceptual learning and motor learning. Perceptual learning enables us to adapt to our environment. As humans, we can recognize things as familiar and readily categorize them in our brains. These circuits also have the ability to change once we have categorized them because of synaptic plasticity. Did you notice that day your professor showed up to class with a new haircut or a new pair of glasses? Soon enough that image you had of them in your head shifts to reflect that change in a process of relearning. This is all taking place in an explicit-thinking cortical brain area known as the striate cortex. Many studies show that damage to this area leaves people unable to recognize familiar stimuli like the faces of their loved ones. For our college students, perceptual learning is extremely important because it helps them interpret and make sense of sensory information from their environment. Perceptual skills can help students more easily encode and retrieve information, making it easier to remember and apply what they've learned. It also helps with identifying patterns, or similarities and differences, in information, which is essential for problem-solving and critical thinking. We may see those students with excellent perceptual skills choosing careers in architecture or physics, where understanding complex visual and spatial relationships is often integral to grasping the major concepts.

Motor learning, on the other hand, is something we do when learning a novel sequence of behavioral patterns. Usually what one would think of in regard to motor skills learned in school would be the pattern of throwing or kicking a ball in athletics, but what about something that all of our millennials seem to be experts at today? Typing—and even more so, texting. We have an area of the brain called the primary motor cortex that is laid out as a big map for motor movement. Despite the complexity of neuroscience, this region is simple. If you were able to experimentally turn on this region in the exact right spot, your pinky would move. If you move slightly lower on the brain and turn that on, then your arm will move. The interesting thing about this map is that it's essentially the same for all of us, and it is mapped in a very similar fashion in our animal counterparts. This primary motor cortex, though, is only one piece of the puzzle; learning a motor movement involves other regions of the brain. Hitting a ball with a bat is much more than a quick mental note that says "Move right arm," as that would just result in a single twitch and not a smooth movement as intended. Thus, we must include additional regions such as the premotor cortex, which helps to integrate sensory information such as the keyboard underneath your fingertips, and the ventral premotor cortex, which is home to cells called "mirror neurons" that allow your body to replicate a movement or a behavior seen in another person.

When learning a motor skill, the initial movements come fast (e.g., fingers or thumbs sliding across a keyboard or a phone). That skill is consolidated in the brain, meaning that the repeated pattern begins to form the neural connections necessary to store it in the brain as a patterned movement. This happens when we can quickly move from that single finger visually searching for a letter on the keyboard to using all fingers to quickly form words on the screen, eventually without even looking. "Practice makes perfect" is absolutely the case in motor learning. After a motor skill is learned, though, it seems we stop getting better at it. Brandy knows that she can type quickly since she learned the skill in middle school, back when the cool thing to do was race your friends on typing games in keyboarding class. But twenty years later, despite using the skill almost every day, she hasn't gotten much better. This is what people refer to as a memory plateau,[2] or the phase in the learning process where an individual's performance seems to stagnate or level off.

In the 1960s, psychologists Paul Fitts and Michael Posner investigated this question and proposed that skill acquisition comes in three phases.[3] The *first phase*, or the "cognitive stage," is what we would refer to as the phase of explicit thinking. During this phase, you intellectualize the task at hand and spend time actively thinking about ways to improve during the task. During the *second phase*, or "associative stage," you are able to become more proficient, making fewer errors with each trial and needing to concentrate less. The *last phase*, called the "autonomous stage," is when that task has moved entirely from explicit thinking to implicit thinking, just like we saw was possible with stimulus-response and perceptual learning. During that autonomous stage, though, the autopilot that your brain is able to run on (which will be discussed in the next section) stays in that plateau. From Fitts's and Posner's work came the coined phrase "okay plateau," or that phase in which your autopilot maintains how good you are at a task.

Again, when it comes Brandy, she is at her "okay plateau" with typing. Sure, she could be better, but she's not challenging herself and her typing ability because her speed gets the work done. If one wants to physically get better at typing or any skill, a successful way to do that is to vary your practice. Switching between focusing on speed versus accuracy and taking the time to identify the words and letters that you physically are typing more slowly and practicing those specifically are all ways to improve. Variations and challenges to the routine that activate explicit thinking are what will help anyone performing motor tasks, even professional athletes, break through motor plateaus and promote continued improvement. Ultimately, to improve that performance, you have to rip that implicit skill out of autopilot and analyze it explicitly. If you don't do that, you'll stay on the okay plateau, a place that we find many of our college students as they continue on a successful autopilot rather than striving for their ultimate potential. A place where a student will never learn that professional wisdom we continue to return to.

## Information Transfer from Explicit to Implicit, or More Specifically, Habit Formation

Stimulus-response, motor, and perceptual learning are all components of the bigger picture. These types of learning are all explicit. They take conscious, active thought. This is why studying for an upcoming exam while scrolling through social media usually does not go well for our college students. That explicit stream likes to focus on one task at a time. The more information that we can get to transfer from our explicit stream to our implicit stream, though, the easier a task at hand is going to be. Think about driving your car. Can you sing along with your favorite song while cruising safely down the road? Or are you that sixteen-year-old sweating, with your heart racing out of your chest, waiting for your father to tell you which way to turn on your way home from school because despite the fact that you have ridden home in the car a thousand times, all of a sudden you can't remember the turns now that your mind is full of thoughts about using your turn signal, how fast to accelerate, and not going one mile per hour over that speed limit? Of course, practice is what helps us move this information between brain circuits and helps us concrete these routine behaviors.

We know that there is no way to shut off the brain. The information that was your active focus while performing that task at hand gets shifted through circuits and replayed, even when you are daydreaming, thinking about nothing, or asleep. Remember that default mode network that we talked about in chapter 3?

One brain region that is critical for the information transfer itself is located deep in the brain and called the striatum. This brain region acts as a hub for encoding sequences of motor movements and the actions associated with those behaviors. The repeated striking of fingers on a keyboard, discussed earlier, becomes ingrained again because our neurons modify their structures and form new connections because the brain is neuroplastic. To dive a little deeper, there is a specific region known as the dorsomedial striatum (that just means it's more toward the middle back region of the brain area) that is critical for active learning. You can't learn a motor task such as tying your shoes without this region. The dorsolateral striatum is an important hub for the execution of habits that are already learned. Here we have a brain region that holds both explicit and implicit functions right next to each other, and we know that these two regions actively talk to each other. Moreover, scientists have shown that they can selectively turn on and off these regions and block learning and habit separately, depending on if they hit that medial area or that lateral area.[4] The ability to transfer information between these regions and through further loops that help coordinate motor movements is what gives this region the ability to automate behaviors over time. As habit becomes more ingrained, the striatum helps execute the behavior more efficiently and with minimal explicit effort.

The striatum is also critical for forming cue-response associations, such as that habitual response of hitting snooze if you're not a morning person or getting out of bed immediately without consciously thinking about it if you are. This might be different on special days where you are off schedule, like when you have to drive to the airport for an early-morning flight and explicitly set that alarm so that you do not have time to hit snooze six times as you might routinely do on a workday. Nonetheless, the striatum is critical for those simple associations of hitting snooze or checking your phone after you hear it go off or vibrate in your pocket. When this region malfunctions, we see abnormal activity that can be associated with obsessive-compulsive disorder, where patients develop compulsive behaviors in response to specific cues. Severe damage to this region, such as what we see in patients that suffer from Parkinson's disease, results in the patient struggling to form new habits and perform new skills.

Maybe the transfer of skills and knowledge (and even thinking skills like memorization) to the dorsomedial striatum is part of building that "mechanic's feel" for the issue that marks someone who is starting to develop professional wisdom from experience.

We have already discussed the importance of dopamine in driving behavior, and the same applies for this circuit. Dopamine plays a vital role in habit formation and reinforcement. This region contains dopamine-releasing neurons that contribute to the rewarding or reinforcing aspects of habitual behaviors. When we receive a reward or experience pleasure after successfully performing a habituated task, dopamine release strengthens the neural pathways associated with that habit—making it more likely to be repeated in the future. As habits develop, this region can influence decision-making. It can bias choices and actions in favor of habits over deliberative, goal-directed behaviors. This can lead to automatic and sometimes less flexible responses wherein a habit is triggered. We can see this habit taking over in our college students when they return to their dorm rooms after a long day of classes, lay down on their bed, put their earbuds in, and turn on the next episode of their favorite Netflix series. It is a habit, it feels good, but sometimes this habitual behavior takes over the need to study for the exam that is coming up the following morning in US History.

## Learning Is Different from Memory

Memorization is a skill that is difficult to master, and some college courses that our students find themselves in rely on this skill. If you've ever taken a course in anatomy and physiology (one of us teaches that class), you likely remember the weeks where you had a list of about a hundred bones and markings on the bones or muscles and where they originate and insert on the human body. While teaching critical thinking is a skill and something that higher education institutions, especially those with a strong liberal arts focus, try to make an integral part of their mission, sometimes the task at hand is simply about transferring that list of bones from short-term to long-term memory so that you can pull it out of the back of your brain the following week to ace that laboratory practical exam.

It is always interesting as a professor to watch these students and the way that they learn. Each semester, there are a few students that can list every bone or muscle by the end of the three hours in the lab and only spend an hour or two outside of class running through the list one more time, and it's concreted in their mind. This is definitely a skill that our talented perceptual learners excel in. Other students, on the other hand, you see in the lab for hours and hours each week, and they struggle to earn a passing grade on the exam despite their efforts. The only thing that these students have in common, as we always tell them, is that if they spend one additional hour the next week studying, then they are very likely to perform even better on the next exam. But that doesn't make the student spending twenty hours a week any less jealous of the student spending two hours a week to earn the same grade.

So, what exactly is underlying this information transfer? Is the ability to memorize a muscle's characteristics able to be trained in the brain? Joshua Foer, author of the book *Moonwalking with Einstein*,[3] would argue that indeed it is. In his book, he delves into the art of memory by immersing himself in the world of competitive memory competitions and learning from memory experts. Foer spent one year training for the USA Memory Championship, and to his surprise, with some intense training and focus set aside for a few hours each day, he was able to come in first place. Foer, who had an average IQ, no previous experience with memory tasks, and started his journey with skepticism about memory training, was able to memorize a full deck of cards in a minute and forty seconds. The thought of a student memorizing fifty-two different bones, like Foer's fifty-two different cards, in under two minutes is simply unfathomable.

What is really interesting about memory, though, is that this skill that Foer was able to learn is not commonly taught or emphasized in modern education and daily life. Perhaps a reason for this is the current dependence on technology. We live in a digital age. The reliance we have on our smartphones to immediately access, store, and retrieve information has essentially phased out our brain's need to do this. A quick way to think about this is asking yourself the simple question of how many phone numbers do you really know? We might be dating ourselves when we talk about a time when we easily could recall at least twenty phone numbers, especially those of loved ones, a home or work phone, or a favorite pizza place that we would order from once a week while growing up. Now, we live in a time where there is no need to store that information in our brain. Rather than having to lug out a phone book, flip through the pages, search through the thousands of alphabetical names, and physically type the actual digits of a number into the phone, we tap a name on our contact list in our cell phone or a link on a company's website. Or, even more technologically savvy, we just ask Alexa or Siri to dial the number for us automatically. We don't even have to pick up a device.

Let's face it, there has been a shift in modern education that places more of an emphasis on teaching critical thinking, problem-solving, and creativity rather than rote memorization. That is why we notoriously see our students struggling in classes such as Anatomy and Physiology. It's a circuit in the brain that has been left underutilized for years, a skill that in a lot of our college students is yet to be harnessed. Furthermore, internships and jobs that our college students and graduates have continue to shift away from rote memorization to social skills such as adaptability, collaboration, and the ability to apply new information rather than simply recalling existing knowledge. Some of the best doctors score low on their medical board exams; some of the best lawyers score low on their bar exam, and some of the best electricians, cosmetologists, social workers, surveyors, and many more score low on their licensing exams. All of these gatekeeping assessments test rote memorization, or the ability of your brain to categorize and retain information. They don't test whether you can treat a client or patient with humility, which is often a huge factor setting the "good" from the "bad" professionals in these spaces. It also does not test your skill, which can of course be a serious issue for some hands-on professions.

Habit is a bit like a memory in that it is stored in the implicit mind. Whereas the striatum acts as that central hub for a motor task, the hippocampus is the brain region important for taking the information we are presented with in a textbook and sticking it into our mind to later regurgitate on an examination.[6] We call this "semantic information." Knowing your birthday would be a good example of this type of material. The hippocampus is the major brain region involved in the initial encoding and acquisition of new factual knowledge by creating a temporary memory representation of that information within its neuronal connections. Again, neuroplasticity makes this possible. Additionally, the hippocampus helps store episodic information, or the facts associated with an event. If I asked you to describe to me what you did last year on your birthday, this would be the part of your memory you hacked into to tell me that you went out to eat at your favorite restaurant with your four best friends from college. After the initial encoding of a fact or details associated with an event, the hippocampus consolidates this information and ships it to long-term storage areas such as the neocortex. In this process, the hippocampus helps strengthen connections between neurons, making memory more stable and less reliant on the hippocampus itself. The hippocampus also communicates and is influenced by many other brain regions, including emotional circuits that hold biases, fears, likes, and dislikes. This integration can influence the emotional significance and salience of memories, making some specific memories much stronger and more vivid than others. While only about ten or so of those bones you learned in lab that day stuck in your head by the time you left, the skeleton toppling over onto your professor and causing them to spill their coffee all over those two students you dislike that never stop talking is a memory that will last a lifetime because you found it hilarious.

## Putting It All Together: Learning and Memory Integration

Again, we are both professors, and anyone who has taught before will be able to relate to that feeling of walking into your classroom on the first day of your first teaching gig. There's a feeling in your stomach, that imposter syndrome, questioning if you're intelligent enough to teach the course and hoping that no one asks a question that stumps you. You run down your attendance sheet and every single name soon escapes your mind. It's only five minutes into the class at this point and you feel like you just won't make the remaining fifty-five minutes, let alone the rest of an entire semester. Fast-forward to the last day of class, or perhaps the first day of class ten years down the line, and if you are lucky, that feeling is long gone. The reason for this is that again, with repetition, we make habits that help us to calm the nerves with a smooth interplay of those implicit patterns we have run through dozens of times and the explicit thoughts of the task at hand. Taking attendance? Easy, and maybe we've even seen some of these students in other courses or had a sibling of theirs. Diving into that first lecture? No sweat. Not only do we know what to expect on the slide; we also know dozens of other interesting and exciting facts stored down in our implicit circuits that we can throw in if the class goes in that direction. Answering questions? Well, as experienced professors, we've absolutely perfected the art of saying, "That is an excellent question," and if we don't know the answer, we'll say something suave like "We don't have time to talk about that today" or "We will get to that in the next lecture," move on, and look up the information later to relay back to the curious student either by email or in the next class.

Learning and memory are heavily intertwined processes. Relational learning is a term referring to the process by which an individual learns the relationship between different stimuli, objects, events, or concepts. It is the process by which our brain puts together stimulus-response, perceptual, and motor learning into fluid processes and stores them using our memory circuits. This integration is essential for understanding and navigating the complex environments that we live in, where recognizing patterns, associations, and the context of elements relative to one another is critical for success and for professional wisdom. Without this ability, our young, college-educated job seekers would not be able to understand and interact with their environment by recognizing and remembering different relationships. To put things simply, they would not be able to integrate that classroom-based knowledge with their task at hand during an internship.

## Summary

In this chapter we have laid out numerous brain regions that play a role in information transfer from our task-at-hand explicit thinking to our habitual unconscious information storage areas. It is important to remember that the names of these brain regions are trivial (or semantic, if you remember that from earlier). What is important to understand, though, is that our brain has the ability to learn in different forms, store information, and integrate this all together. Moreover, it can modify these circuits through its neuroplasticity. Understanding this as an institution of higher education is critical for creating students that are able to not only recite facts but also bring this information into practice in a hands-on setting. In the next chapters, we will be moving away from how our brain accomplishes these amazing tasks to focus on how brain functioning relates to professional wisdom and what higher education is doing and should be doing to cultivate this in their students.

Chapter 6

# Higher Education Structure and the Development of Professional Wisdom

Clearly, the concept of professional wisdom is important to this book; it is in the title. We think we've coined this term. And if you've made it this far, you know we also think that professional wisdom is a product of the mix of explicit and implicit learning in college and that each primarily affects different parts of the brain. Explicit learning is what we think of when we think of college: getting content knowledge, making the choice of classes that support majors and minors, having a career after graduation. Implicit learning, we would argue, is particularly strong when a student does an internship or some other direct experience in their field of interest and the experience lets them apply that explicit learning to get a feel for the career or field. This concept of feeling is what happens when the limbic system or emotions react to the real-world experience, and it adds a value judgment to the cognitive knowledge gained there as well as in college classroom learning.

Let's go back to something we said earlier and define professional wisdom by what it is not. It is not cynicism. When the famous writer Oscar Wilde said a cynic is someone "who knows the price of everything and the value of nothing," he gave us that definition by contrast. In college, we teach students in largely facts-and-theories classrooms. It is a highly efficient process, and one that has been refined over centuries. Many academics would agree now that this system of higher education is full of students who are excellent at memorizing and giving back information on an exam. But some fear that we are not generating "wise" graduates—maybe ones who are not cynical, per se, but at least not wise in their intended fields. How do we avoid that?

Facts and theories are cognitive input, pure information transfer bouncing between processing brain circuits over to storage regions—just what we needed before information technology gave us the ability to store things in massive quantities outside of the brain. If it is the emotional process that gives students the value piece, it is the history and practice of higher education that eliminates much emotion on the basis of efficiency of cognitive input and of tradition.

Here is where students call colleges and universities the "ivory tower," and we take that as an expression of the isolation students can feel from the university and the professors who teach there. Why? In today's world, facts and theories are at everyone's fingertips or nearby in someone's purse or pocket. So one could ask, why do we even need professors? Or for that matter, why do we need college at all? We think the answer is that something else is happening besides the cognitive transfer of information, something that keeps students coming to higher education and, importantly for us, paying for higher education. We think it is the emotional input, the self-discovery, and the space to do some growing up. While most of us agree with that idea, up until now it has not broadly infiltrated the teaching systems in most colleges. An upgrade is overdue.

If we look at how exactly we got here, besides just the longstanding tradition, the answer comes (or it can come) from the professors, instructors, lecturers, graduate students, and whomever else we find teaching in our college classrooms. Perhaps you've heard the old adage that a painter is someone who "works to live and lives to paint." Professors are like painters. They fell in love with a field (in the case of your coauthors, it was neuroscience), and they love to study and talk about it—sometimes even dominating far too many holiday party conversations when they go on and on about it, much like many artists or other people who are passionate about their work. When a young assistant professor starts out in their job, they have that passion from spending the last five or more years in a doctorate program plus potentially another five or more years in a postdoctoral fellowship (e.g., if they are in our field of neuroscience). But these young professors also have more of a relationship or commonality with the other young people at a college, like students. Many students would argue that it is easier to connect with the young faculty on campus than those who have been tenured for many years. An ability to connect with a professor and the material they are teaching is what sparks that emotion and passion in the student, arguably in the best way possible to teach: by example.

With a passionate professor and engaged students, everything becomes possible. Students push themselves to do better because of their affection for the teacher and for the subject. They can be encouraged to practice producing new knowledge through essay tests and papers, even though they are more demanding forms of evaluation than typical multiple-choice tests. They can be persuaded to work in teams even when it is a challenge to organize the group and collaborate on projects, integrating multiple perspectives into a conversation. We professors can get them to present orally to other students even when they would rather be quiet, challenging and encouraging the public speaking skills they will need to interview and land that dream job. Most importantly, we can get them to critically think while discussing complex topics with others who might challenge them, even when it is easier to just memorize and regurgitate information from the course textbook.

Professional wisdom emerges from all of these practices, and there is a growing body of evidence to say that these are "high-impact" practices in the classroom for this reason. Through them, as with experiential education, students can get a feel for the field of study, not just the facts and theories. Over the four years of an undergraduate degree, most do grow and become wiser about the discipline, even if it is not to the extent we would like to see. Nonetheless, it is there. We professors can often see it emerge even though it is a challenge to directly measure.

Let's go a little deeper here.

## The Professor and the Process of Higher Education

In our opinion, a problem with professors and teaching in the institution begins with a good thing: when the demands of successful scholarship start to grow for them. Young professors are already deeply interested in the research of their fields, and universities need them to be that way. It is what generally separates high school from college: that expertise that involves a much greater depth and many more years of schooling. It is a shift from knowing what is in the textbook to being the person who writes the chapters of the textbook. Graduate students must engage in knowledge discovery to earn their doctoral degree and then continue with that success in order to move up the academic ladder and eventually become the coveted tenured professor. Their research and scholarly discoveries give a university a reputation that is not only prestigious but also attracts students who pay tuition and keep the college afloat.

When a brand-new assistant professor is first on campus, they tend to better balance that research passion with a natural excitement for the students in their classes. They see themselves in those students and want to inspire them in whatever ways similarly inspired them to fall in love with the field. But navigating this heavy load is a challenge. Jim specifically remembers that when he took his first job at Harvard University in the Psychology Department, his well-meaning graduate faculty told him to not pay too much attention to the undergraduates in his classes or they would "line up outside your door and seek discussion or even mentoring with you." They told him then that the Harvard undergraduates were starved for real professorial attention and cautioned that these wonderful students would "take the time that you need for your research." It was of course interesting advice for any new professor to receive, but hopefully you can see the issues with it.

To earn tenure, the new professor is faced with a pressing need to establish themselves in a field made up of much older, more successful senior professors with resumes that go on for pages and pages. These senior professors invite the new professors to give talks at conferences they are organizing or submit papers to journals they are editing as an opportunity to review the new professors. Or these senior professors will sit in judgment of the young professors' grant applications and decide the fate of their careers that are dependent on securing funding and publishing. They then are the ones that take seats as reviewers of a young professor's tenure portfolio to scrutinize if the applicant's performance is up to the standard that they think it should be for their academic institution. So, in this long-standing, traditional academic world, a professor spending as much time as possible doing research, securing grants, and publishing to get tenure is paramount and often comes at the expensive of teaching at their highest level. Since the professoriate is the center of gravity of the department-level management of any university, this attitude tends to pervade the system, even for those who are not on a tenure track or tenured.

The process of serving on a tenure committee or as a senior administrator is not necessarily the most fun for the tenured professor either. Jim remembers reviewing hundreds of cases for promotion over twenty years as an administrator and was well known for saying that it seemed to him that the most tense people on the faculty were the assistant professors in the last two years before the tenure decision. As most people outside the university system do not know, failure to get tenure means that the candidate is fired the following year. No office, no salary, no studio or laboratory, and a ding to one's reputation that is enough to make any person nervous. With the extremely competitive nature of academia—especially within the past few years, with declining numbers of doctorally trained applicants being produced—falling back into the academic job market at this point is not a welcome option for anyone. So, it is perhaps understandable if they pull away some from their initial investment in teaching and prioritize what the tenure committee reviewers are looking most closely at, which surprisingly isn't a professor's student evaluations—at least not at a university promoting its research capacity.

One would think, then, that after earning tenure, things would get much better and the faculty member could devote more time to their classroom teaching commitments. After all, that tremendous pressure of losing one's job is gone. But what we are more likely to see is that the senior professor, who is accomplished in their field and in demand for publications and talks, may begin to look at undergraduates as a time sink rather than seeing those students as precious charges they must teach and nurture. Professors at this level are now tasked with defending their reputations, and the pressure continues. At the next conference, they are expected to have new data to show and an active body of productive student researchers in their laboratory. If you ask a professor who they are, they will often describe themselves first by their field.

We, your coauthors, do that ourselves. If you stop and ask us who we are, we might respond by saying we are neuroscientists. Then we could add our institution and maybe our position and what we teach. This is exactly what the university wants. They want us to put research first. Otherwise, they would not have hired a research scholar in the first place or allowed them to continue to develop that scholarship about which the institution will then brag. It is all perfectly natural when you look at it from an administrative standpoint. But it is potentially deleterious in its effect on students and that must be recognized, especially if the students start to feel they are in the ivory tower, where the institution cares less about them. We will discuss that a bit later.

A typical student who is the subject of this process sees their professors only in lecture halls, some of these lecture halls being quite large, with hundreds of other students. If the professor is at a large research institution, they may have graduate students that set up the lecture, answer the questions after, and do the grading. Oftentimes these lectures are absolutely brilliant, depending on the institution you are at, but they also can seem a bit distant from the daily experience of the undergraduate. If the student needs advice on course selection for the next semester, they go to their academic advisor. If they want to explore an internship in the field they are studying, they go see the career services office or maybe join a departmental student club focused on the major. If they have a question about the course material, they know to meet with a graduate teaching assistant or a student who has completed the course and is now working in the university's tutoring center.

What we also tend to see is that these busy, research-focused professors often tend to use multiple-choice or other standardized tests that can be entirely or largely machine graded. The university typically maintains an office where the graduate students can drop off a stack of printed answer sheets from the course exams and get back grades and a distribution of class performance. The process is highly fair, but again, it is not natural. When was the last time someone asked you a question in life and gave you a list of potential multiple-choice answers? Life is an essay test and critical thinking is required, not just the memorization of facts and picking out the "best" answer from a choice of four presented to you. But creating a test that challenges a student's ability to integrate and apply the course material, especially in a written format, takes a lot of time, and grading it takes even more. In this academic world, time is capital and something that a professor at any stage in their career cannot afford to waste. Time for teaching undergraduate students is what this aspect of the process has too often ground out of the enthusiastic young assistant professor.

The professors that fall victim to this process are not bad people, but this kind of a methodical process development over time depends upon us not noticing. As we like to say in our classes on the neuroscience of sensory adaptation, none of you sitting here reading this book feel your underwear. You did when you first put it on, but since it has not hurt you yet, the brain adapts so you can turn your attention to watching out for cars when crossing the street or concentrating on what you are reading without distraction. The same happens to young professors who are enthusiastic about their students—or at least to some of them. There are of course older professors who remain empathetic and even happy and are great teachers as well as good scholars. Some professors (including us) even invite undergraduate students to work with them on their scholarship and thus give them an out-of-class, internship-like educational experience in the university and greatly enjoy doing this. These experiences are pivotal for the undergraduates that want to continue on to a research position or graduate school, but they may be a challenge to find and are often very competitive. It is also fun for the undergraduate students to do work at the graduate student level in any field with a professor's group. Those students are a minority of the population, and they are the lucky ones.

## The Ivory Tower of Higher Education

One allure of small colleges is they don't have the same ivory tower association as larger universities. Students expect to feel less like just a number at these institutions because of their smaller size, and they hope to foster relationships with professors that know their names and can write impactful letters of recommendation. At these schools, you will see a slightly different balance between research and teaching in the institution's mission.

At both colleges and universities, students view the classroom as a familiar place. One that is comfortable, even if it can sometimes be a bit less personally engaging than they hoped. In our experience, the students like and respect that so much of classroom teaching is organized in advance so that fairness rules and surprise and stress are minimized. The syllabus says when exams occur, how much they are worth to the overall grade, the topics of each day and week, and generally what can be expected. Both professors and students have adapted to this model as the dominant one, and few question it. Classes, to the university, are like the roads to a city. They are just there, and they structure how you travel through it. The idea that the classroom actually works optimally to educate students can be left out of the institution's thinking. It is tradition and can be very financially efficient when hundreds of students are placed in one lecture section, especially when all of these students are paying the same tuition as those at a smaller school with only twenty other students in the classroom. With the cost of tuition being so high, no one wants to make education less efficient.

It is hard to change the dominant model when it is influenced by these large traditional and economic forces. It is particularly challenging at the department level, out of which classroom teaching is deployed and where professors are in charge as department chairs and as senior faculty. Administration, appropriately, usually stays out of such arrangements. The scholars know best, and there is a hierarchy there that does not bode well for change. As the senior faculty transition into roles of high impact on department structure, such as department chair and dean (or higher), they often favor tradition rather than ingenuity. This is largely why changes that seem so trivial to students in the depths of their academic journey are never heard or acknowledged by departmental leadership. This causes a lot of stagnance in the academic world, even though the professors may be very innovative themselves in their scholarship.

Internships and experiential learning opportunities are ways that a student can break free from the classroom setting and these imposed limitations. This must start, though, with desire by the student to do so, or potentially a college graduation requirement. Students may not say it or even realize it until later in their educational journeys, but they want skills, and they know that as informative as the college environment is, some skills are best learned in the workplace. They do say they want a good resume, which everyone knows is needed for a job after graduation. All seem to know that it is good to have some experience within the field first. All students say they want a better life after they graduate than they would have had if they did not go to college, whether through the following job or entrance into a professional education. That is enough to drive the other side of learning; learning from experience in a way that complements college studies, we hope.

## The Dichotomy of Education and Experience in Higher Education

Slowly but surely, colleges are increasingly judged on their ability to produce skilled graduates. We think that researchers such as Michelle Van Noy, the current director of the Education and Employment Research Center at Rutgers,[1] would agree that this is a challenging metric, but the work needs to be done. In a recent interview with Inside Higher Ed, she discusses the links between education and employment and how slowly higher education is shifting to make this a priority.[2] However, studying this is incredibly difficult because there is intense field-by-field variation, differences between different types of colleges and universities, two-year and four-year programs, and so on. Despite the lag, however, she does state that they have noted an overall responsiveness at the national level.

Given that this research is being done when there is an increasing focus on whether higher education is worth the cost or if it is able to produce employable graduates, it is clear that higher education needs to be examined under a new lens. Conversations up to this point seem to focus on either vocationalism and transferable job skills or education in its purest form. We would argue that higher education is responsible for finding a middle ground between these two things. This dichotomy is doing more harm than good, as there are increasing arguments about the current skills-based hiring movement and how higher education is responding to this. We will speak more to this in chapter 11, but again we are back at professional wisdom, or the implicit and explicit relationships between knowledge and skill.

## So, How Does Experiential Education Develop Professional Wisdom?

The answer to that question may come from a 2011 book called *Practical Wisdom* by Schwartz and Sharpe.[3] In the opening, they talk about how most jobs have rules that employees must follow and incentives to keep those workers adhering to them. They say this reduces the likelihood of someone going off track (and it reminds us of the well-defined college experience). It also tends to reduce the development of practical wisdom. They give an example of a janitor in a hospital who had just cleaned a patient's room when the father returned and insisted that he had not done so. Rather than argue with the parent and keep himself on schedule (i.e., following the rules), the janitor decided to clean the room again, in part because the father was already upset in response to his child's illness. In this instance, we see the opposite of our college student sitting in the classroom, potentially learning how to diagnose and save that child. Rather, we see a man hired for a skill that does not necessarily require an academic backbone. This man, though, shows his wisdom in how he understands the mission of the hospital: to take care of patients and their families. He was able to integrate his skills with his emotional knowledge in what we would argue is a practically wise response. If you remember our discussion on brain circuits, he was able to integrate implicit feelings about the situation with explicit actions. This is what employers want to see. Oftentimes employers can fall short in having too many guardrails to keep people from steering out of their clearly developed lanes and accessing these important circuits.

We see another aspect of this in the book *Zen and the Art of Motorcycle Maintenance* by Robert Pirsig,[4] which is nominally a story about a father and son motorcycle trip across the country, but in our opinion it is really about how one takes life lessons from experiences. At one point, the father is putting a screw into the cowl of his motorcycle after repairing the engine, and he thinks about how he knows just how much torque to put on the screw that will make it firmly stay in place but also not strip the threads. How does he know that? It comes from having had either or both of those mistakes happen from prior attempts. There is no torque dial on the screwdriver that tells you how hard to turn. Explaining in words to someone who has never done this is extremely challenging. It depends on that feeling that you get with experience. You just know. Felt knowledge in the implicit neurocircuitry of the mechanic is just as important as the experience our college student gets at the hand of their mentor during an experiential learning opportunity.

Professional wisdom is the integration of our janitor's skills with the felt knowledge of our mechanic in these examples. In our college students, direct experiences can nurture this integration of implicit and explicit thought, motivated through what feels right and what feels wrong. Our current higher education system gives students an immense variety of choices that are based on feel. This begins with the location, type of school, prestige, and other variables, and extends in much greater depth through choices about field of study, courses to take, and out-of-classroom experiences while still a student. What they like to do, want to do, and need to do in order to earn a living following graduation are all important considerations that every college student makes—as does the college itself in marketing and trying to secure students to attend the institution. Colleges respond to these considerations by trying to provide information and guide students to a positive course of decisions, but ultimately, these choices belong to the student. We can only hope they make ones that are professionally wise.

Years after graduation, alumni often say, "I wish I knew then what I know now." It is easier later in life to integrate those experiences and education into that ultimate feel that we believe to underlie professional wisdom. There is a value to the student being able to accomplish this level of maturity before graduation, as they can better identify, seek, and secure the job that keeps their explicit brain excited, interested, and motivated while utilizing the knowledge, skills, and passion that have been developed and stored in the implicit circuitry. We believe the higher education system has a responsibility to create an environment that either encourages or requires some skills-based training alongside traditional didactic experience. If higher education is not able to meet somewhere in the middle between these two, the job market is going to suffer, as we will be graduating many students that arguably are not professionally wise.

## Summary

The linear structure of higher education does not create professional wisdom in a student on its own for many reasons. This starts with professors in that they typically begin their careers enthusiastic about teaching undergraduates, but the incremental effects of doing research for job advancement minimizes their time with students. Again, this is not true for all professors—true masters of teaching exist and actively work at it—but it is an unfortunate effect of the traditional ivory tower structure of universities. Students can feel as though exceptional work is required to garner the attention of faculty, which goes against the purpose of education. Exceptional minds must be cultivated, not used on occasion. Again and again, we see that when students learn, perhaps implicitly or at a gut level or even emotionally, that effect combines with cognitive knowledge to produce the beginning of professional wisdom. Learning from experience is brain-natural, a function directly representative of its adaptive survival structure. To truly create a professionally wise college graduate, the strong split between vocationalism and traditional academics must be demolished. From this, a new ground where our colleges and universities blend these two perspectives together can emerge, which is something that would make the academics and employers quite pleased.

Chapter 7

# Intelligence and How Best to Learn Inside and Outside of the Classroom

Defining intelligence is not an easy task, as it is a multifaceted concept that varies based on context. Many individuals would say that the astrophysicist researching life on different planets is much more intelligent than the plumber coming to your home to fix your leaking faucet, or that if someone holds an advanced degree, they are more intelligent than the individual that did not graduate from high school. More and more, we are seeing a push away from the skilled trades and into higher education despite an increasing need for vocationalist or blue-collar careers that are rewarding and sustaining financially.

For many, there is a feeling that higher education is the pipeline to the American dream. But many people prove this wrong. Take Bill Gates for example, the Harvard dropout who now has a net worth over one hundred billion dollars. Maybe this is an extreme case, but he along with others such as Mark Zuckerberg, Steve Jobs, Ralph Lauren, and even Rachael Ray do not hold any sort of undergraduate degree. Yet you are familiar with them despite this. Unarguably, all of these individuals are extremely intelligent and, as we would say, professionally wise, but what exactly does that mean and how does it overlap? As we will discuss later, IBM is now hiring about half of its workforce based on skills, not degrees.[1]

## An Attempt at Defining Intelligence

Everyone defines intelligence in a different manner. The simplest perspective would be that of general cognitive ability. Our typical test for this is going to be an intelligence quotient (or IQ) test. If you've never taken one, these tests typically focus on spatial recognition, short-term memory, mathematical ability, and analytical thinking. These tests have received much scrutiny, though, as they come with many limitations. For example, these tests often reflect cultural knowledge and the values of the society in which they were developed. This can be a huge disadvantage for individuals from different cultural or socioeconomic backgrounds. It would only make sense that our astrophysicist would score much higher in this measure than our plumber. Also, these tests primarily evaluate certain types of cognitive abilities, such as logical reasoning, mathematical skills, and verbal comprehension. They often overlook other forms of intelligence, such as creative, practical, or emotional intelligence. When it comes to our college majors, one study showed that physics, mathematics, economics, and philosophy are among the highest-IQ majors, whereas education, social work, and psychology are at the bottom of this list.[2] That doesn't bode well for us neuroscience/psychology educators writing this book.

Howard Gardner, a developmental psychologist, proposed the theory of multiple intelligences in his 1983 book *Frames of Mind: The Theory of Multiple Intelligences*.[3] His theory challenges the traditional view of intelligence as a single, general ability and instead suggests that humans possess a variety of distinct intelligences. According to Gardner, these intelligences are relatively independent of each other, and individuals may excel in one or more areas while being average or below average in others. These types of intelligence include linguistic, logical-mathematical, spatial, musical, bodily-kinesthetic, intrapersonal, interpersonal, and naturalistic. We all possess these intelligences to varying degrees. Yet we are still limited in our definition, as even within the whole group of astrophysicists or plumbers out there, there is a huge range of diversity. Gardner's theory of multiple intelligences did have a significant impact on education and psychology, encouraging a more holistic and personalized approach to learning and development. It emphasizes the importance of recognizing and nurturing diverse talents and abilities in individuals rather than focusing solely on traditional measures of intelligence, such as IQ tests, something that we must keep in mind as college educators with a historically strong academic slant in our teaching.

Daniel Goleman, a psychologist and science journalist, popularized the concept of emotional intelligence (EI) with his 1995 book *Emotional Intelligence: Why It Can Matter More Than IQ*.[4] Goleman's work built on earlier research by psychologists Peter Salovey and John D. Mayer, who first introduced the term "emotional intelligence" in the early 1990s. Goleman expanded and popularized the concept, highlighting its importance in various aspects of life, including personal relationships, professional success, and overall well-being. In this theory, there were five key components: self-awareness, self-regulation, motivation, empathy, and social skills.

As individuals who persevered through PhD programs, your coauthors are very familiar with the notion that earning the degree is just as much about academic performance as a value of intelligence as it is about the motivation to get through the program. The term "grit" has become very popular to describe this sort of intelligence that is more about self-perseverance and discipline than pure brilliance.[5] One well-known professor, Angela Duckworth, became famous for studying this trait at West Point and showing that it played a key role in the persistence of those students. She wrote a book about it.[6]

While having a credential is a quick and easy way for a hiring agency to deem someone "intelligent," Goleman's theory would argue that emotional intelligence is just as important, if not more so, than traditional measures of intelligence (such as IQ) for success in various domains of life. High emotional intelligence can enhance personal relationships, improve leadership abilities, and contribute to overall mental and emotional well-being—all traits that we see in our field leaders, from the lead NASA astrophysicists to the lead union plumbers.

Robert Sternberg, yet another psychologist, proposed the triarchic theory of intelligence,[7] which suggests that intelligence is composed of three interrelated aspects: analytical, creative, and practical intelligence. Sternberg's theory challenges the traditional view of intelligence as a single, general ability and offers a more comprehensive understanding of how individuals use their cognitive abilities in various contexts. One component of this is analytical or componential intelligence. This involves the ability to analyze, judge, compare, and contrast. It's similar to a traditional IQ measure in that it would assess problem-solving, logic, critical thinking, and academic ability. The second component is creative or experiential intelligence, which involves the ability to generate new ideas and deal with novel situations. We like to call this "thinking outside of the box," which is arguably a challenging intelligence to both teach and measure academically. The third component is practical or contextual intelligence. This involves the ability to adapt to and select environments that meet one's goals. We like to call this "common sense," or in some instances "street smarts."

This third component is critical for teamwork, managing others, and solving practical problems in daily life that often involve the correct interpretation and response to social cues. Sternberg's triarchic theory is interesting in that it emphasizes that intelligence is not just about processing information but also about how effectively individuals can apply their cognitive abilities in different contexts. According to

Sternberg, traditional IQ tests often fail to capture the full range of human intelligence because they primarily focus on analytical skills and overlook creative and practical abilities, or those components of practical wisdom that we argue are desired by hiring managers. He even wrote a book about wisdom.[8]

One more theory of intelligence that uniquely does not come from a psychologist but rather a former drummer: Robert Hamilton, of the early 1990s Irish rock band The Fat Lady Sings.[9] It is called "sympathetic intelligence." The origins of this theory and the emerging Center for Sympathetic Intelligence[10] lie within the fact that as a drummer, he had a unique vantage point on the world from behind his bandmates and their huge audiences. He describes the atmosphere of the venue as "palpable," where he could feel the connection between himself, the band, and the audience members despite them being from different backgrounds. One could go as far as calling it a "collective epiphany." This sort of synchronicity or connectivity occurred when everyone locked into the beat of the music. He termed that reaction "sympathetic intelligence" to emphasize the connection or resonance between people that gives them the ability to understand and share the feelings of others. To be sympathetically intelligent, there is a social aspect in which emotional regulation as well as understanding interpersonal relationships is key. After all, humans are social creatures, so this linking of the gut (emotional feel), mind (cognitive feel), and heart (seeking that need to interact with others) makes sense, and when done correctly this can give groups a sense of togetherness and belonging.

Other theories and definitions of intelligence definitely exist. There are biological and neurological perspectives that focus on intelligence as a result of brain structure and function, meaning neural efficiency, brain volume, and the speed of neural transmission. There are cultural perspectives that emphasize social harmony, community involvement, and practical problem-solving over the cognitive tasks our primary, secondary, and higher education systems currently focus on. There are also behavioral approaches that try to define intelligence as a set of behaviors and skills that can be observed and measured. With all of that, it is important to understand that intelligence expands far beyond cognitive abilities. Emotional and practical abilities must also be taken into consideration. This has huge implications for educators in that teaching and evaluation should encompass a broader range of skills and abilities beyond those typically measured in our educational system. By fostering analytical, creative, and practical skills, particularly through direct experiences, educators can help students develop a more holistic and adaptive form of intelligence, or practical wisdom (skills-based wisdom), that better prepares them for real-world challenges.

## Understanding Different Styles of Learning

With it being a challenge to settle on a perfect definition of intelligence, it is of course a bigger challenge to identify the best methods of cultivating intelligence in our learners. While we will make suggestions for higher education in chapter 11 of this book, we must first look at how individuals learn differently. This allows us to express different forms of intelligence that drive intrinsic gut feelings such as "I like this" or "I don't like this." We need to know how these differences motivate our college learners to work harder in specific areas, keep their motivation and focus, and ultimately gain what the professor wants to see: a better understanding of the topic and an ability to critically analyze the material presented. Maybe that reaction even leads them to the choice of a specific internship where they can get the hands-on experience that we would argue is a critical accompaniment to the classroom material necessary to create professional wisdom.

In all levels of education, we can see different learners. Some students excel with hands-on activities, some excel with solitary learning, some are great at problem-solving but poor in music class, and so on. We see this in our students as they tend to pick majors that just seem to "click" with them. If the student didn't understand biology and chemistry in high school because the course laboratories were just not for them, it is very unlikely that they would select chemical engineering as their college major. While we as undergraduate professors prefer to have students that are curious about and engaged with the material for whatever reason, it is important to know that just presenting the material in one format is not going to reach every learner, despite the student being extremely passionate about the subject. Thus, we believe that it is the role of the educator to be aware of these different styles of learning and see how to engage a diverse audience of learners. More evidence is coming out about the impact of multimodal teaching, but before we talk about that, first we will discuss several specific different styles of learning.

## Visual Learners

These are individuals who understand and retain information better when it is presented in a visual format. It is estimated that approximately 65 percent of the population falls into this category.[11] Visual learners tend to think in images and pictures and benefit from seeing concepts in diagram form. In the undergraduate classroom we sometimes see visual learners benefiting from charts, diagrams, videos, and maps in the lessons. Oftentimes when meeting with these students during office hours for review, creating study tools such as concept maps and using an array of colored pens and highlighters helps the information stick. Flash cards are also a good study tool for our visual learners.

Studies have also shown that visual learners typically have a more active and developed visual cortex, which is the specific brain region responsible for processing visual information. This allows them to efficiently process and interpret visual stimuli.[12] Studies have shown that visual learners have increased gray matter density in the visual cortex areas as well as more efficient pathways that connect different regions of the brain involved in visual processing and integration.[13] Finally, there is increased activity in the parietal lobe (the lobe that deals with spatial sense) during spatial function tasks, and that allows our visual learners to make better visual-spatial relationships.[14]

## Auditory Learners

Does this sound like you? If not, that's alright. But if you much prefer to listen to lectures, debate topics, and enjoy a challenging conversation, you fall with the 30 percent of individuals that are deemed auditory learners.[15] These learners can absorb up to 75 percent of what they hear,[16] which can be enhanced in many ways. One way is through the use of audio recordings of lectures, instructions, and study materials. These learners may enjoy and benefit from educational podcasts and audiobooks. Auditory learners also thrive when more verbal instruction, discussion, and oral presentations are incorporated into lessons.

Group work and study groups also give these students time to reinforce their learning through verbal interaction. If you've seen a student reading aloud from their notes or the textbook or repeating information aloud to summarize key points verbally, they are likely auditory learners. As professors, we are both very big fans of employing mnemonic devices, rhymes, and songs to help memorize facts and concepts. These auditory tools can make learning more engaging and memorable.

If you've ever taken a neuroscience or anatomy course, there's a good chance you know exactly what we are talking about when we say OOOTTAFVGVSH.[17] It is a mnemonic for remembering the twelve paired cranial nerves that exit the nervous system directly from the brain. There are many other catchy mnemonics, some of which are more appropriate to a general audience than others. Distractions are typically very detrimental for our auditory learners: Sounds in the room, whether it be a ticking clock, a student nearby chewing gum, or a noisy air vent, take a student's mind off of the lecture and drop that retention rate of information down much lower. For our auditory learners, it is important to repeat information, as the brain regions and neural mechanisms involved in auditory learning are specialized for receiving, interpreting, and storing auditory information. Specifically, the auditory cortex in the temporal lobe plays a crucial role in detecting and interpreting sounds.

Nearby is Wernicke's area, an area critical for language comprehension, and a bit further forward in the brain is Broca's area, an area critical for speaking and language production.[18] Auditory information is encoded into short-term and long-term memory through the hippocampus and other memory-related regions. This allows auditory learners to recall spoken information and sounds later. Musicians, with their enhanced skill at recognizing pitch, tone, and other characteristics of music that are important for any instrumentalist or vocalist, typically fall into the category of auditory learners. As expected, in this group of individuals, researchers have noted a higher auditory cortex, specifically with this area containing 130 percent more gray matter than in nonmusicians.[19] This facilitates the ease with which our auditory learners excel in verbal skills, have good memories for sounds like lectures or conversations, and hold a preference for listening, as they retain information better when they hear it rather than see it.

## Kinesthetic Learners

If neither the visual nor auditory learner really sound like you, there's a chance that you fall within the remaining 5 percent of people who are classified as kinesthetic learners. These learners, otherwise known as tactile or touch learners, learn best by doing and engaging in physical activities rather than listening to lectures or reading. They have excellent motor memory and recall information better when they incorporate physical movement into their learning process. With that, they may find it challenging to sit still for extended periods of time because of high energy levels. Movement is what helps them focus and retain information, though that leg shaking or pen clicking that brings them into focus may be the exact thing that is driving our auditory learner two seats away crazy and distracting them from the lecture. With lectures, it is difficult for us as professors to create an environment that incorporates movement, but in lab-based courses, we really see integration of that hands-on opportunity. Courses such as organic chemistry tend to click with our kinesthetic learners when they are introduced to the hands-on molecular models used in the lab. A positive correlation actually has been shown in the literature between chemistry test scores and being a kinesthetic learner.[20] This can transfer to other lab-based science courses, especially ones like anatomy, where it is extremely important to get a student's hands on the bones to feel all of the bone markings and see the articulation points rather than just viewing an image of the bone.

This last point leads to many questions about the impact of virtual learning, but again we will discuss that more in chapter 8. Physical note-taking is also a benefit for kinesthetic learners, as the mechanics of writing enforce a stronger imprint on the brain. Studies have shown that as we are shifting from the classic pen and paper to digital note-taking, although speed and efficiency can be increased in regard to recording notes verbatim, the ability to recall this information when assessed later is decreasing.[21] This could perhaps be because of the fact that the note-taker is not challenged to process and reframe the information prior to putting it down or because of the more specific neural mechanisms of kinesthetic learning. These mechanisms link the motor cortex and cerebellum together to create and store motor memories, enhancing learning through action. The somatosensory cortex processes tactile feedback from physical interactions with objects, while the parietal lobes handle proprioceptive feedback (the sense of body position and movement). This sensory input is crucial for kinesthetic learners to understand and remember information. The basal ganglia are key to forming procedural memories, which are memories for how to perform tasks and actions. Through practice and repetition, kinesthetic learners develop strong procedural memories that aid in information acquisition. Research has also shown that combining kinesthetic learning with a self-explaining task, meaning asking for step-by-step verbalization during the learning experience, creates a higher retention rate and depth of learning.[22]

**Other Types**

While these are three of the major learning styles researched by current educational scientists, other styles do exist. Reading/writing learners have been proposed to learn best through interacting with text-based materials. These students much prefer written instructions, use of books and articles, note-taking, summarizing, and written assignments. Logical learners prefer tasks such as math problems and learn best through reasoning and problem-solving. Puzzles, structured reasoning exercises, and step-by-step processes keep these students engaged and retaining information at the highest level. Interpersonal learners, or social learners, learn best through group work, discussions, and collaborative projects. You may find these students doing peer learning or group activities, and we often see them stepping up as much-appreciated tutors for courses. Intrapersonal learners are those you would never see in a group study session. This type of learner has a strong sense of self-motivation and through independent study retains the information presented at a high rate. Musical learners prefer rhythm, music, and sound. We can see these students obviously excelling with musical instruments but also potentially using music as a study tool to enhance their learning environment or studying to the beat of music to help with memory retention. We have to admit to seeing some very creative songs and rhymes to remember information coming out of our courses. Again, these are just some of the theories on types of learners, but it is important to note that college professors have a responsibility to combine multiple modalities of teaching in their classroom if they want to reach the largest number of students possible.

## Diversity and Neurodiversity in Student Learners

Some argue that the previously noted teaching modalities are an oversimplification of learning and that many studies have failed to provide strong empirical evidence supporting the effectiveness of tailoring instruction to specific learning styles. Research often does not show a significant improvement in learning outcomes when instruction is matched to students' preferred learning styles. But acknowledging learning styles acknowledges differences in individual students and their unique preferences. While learning styles should not be the sole focus of educational strategies, incorporating an understanding of these preferences can offer several benefits. By using learning styles as one tool among many, educators can create more dynamic, inclusive, and effective learning environments. This approach acknowledges individual differences and promotes a variety of instructional methods that can cater to the diverse needs of students.

Neurodiversity is a concept that recognizes and appreciates the wide range of neurological differences that exist among individuals. The term "neurodiverse" or "neurodiversity" emerged in the 1990s from an autistic sociologist named Judy Singer,[23] and from this followed a movement called the "neurodiversity movement." It aimed to increase the inclusion of all people, embracing any neurological differences.[24] The concept of neurodiversity challenges the traditional view of "normal" versus "abnormal" brain function, instead promoting the idea that neurological variations, such as autism, ADHD, dyslexia, and others, are natural and valuable forms of human diversity. Higher education is coming to recognize neurodiversity and has a responsibility to create an inclusive learning environment where all students, regardless of their neurological makeup, can thrive academically and socially.

The neurodiversity perspective encourages a broader understanding of intelligence beyond traditional IQ tests, which often fail to capture the full spectrum of cognitive abilities, especially in neurodivergent individuals. Oftentimes, neurodiverse individuals can bring a perspective to a problem-solving situation that conventional-thinking students may not. Solely looking at performance on standardized testing and constant underestimation of these individuals is a detriment in the undergraduate setting. It is not uncommon for these students to have strengths beyond that of the traditional student. Internship settings can oftentimes help develop and highlight these strengths.

Companies including Walgreens, Amazon, and Wawa have more recently created training programs solely for neurodiverse individuals, understanding that individuals with neurodiversity are a pool of untapped talent, with more than half of neurodiverse young adults and 30–40 percent of neurodiverse adults currently being unemployed according to CNBC (a rate three to four times higher than individuals with other disabilities).[25] Walgreens in particular has developed a thirteen-week, hands-on training program to help neurodiverse individuals identify and further develop their job-related skills. Wawa utilizes a system of paired job coaching where neurodivergent employees are paired with a mentor that helps them develop expertise in their role. Amazon has specific training for job recruiters that focuses on the relationship between time investment in an individual and the potential financial and other payoffs that are very comparable if not sometimes more lucrative than neurotypical hires. As companies realize the value of neurodivergence and that it may not necessarily be measured by numbers and traditional metrics, higher education must keep up with this.

The traditional classroom setting is not designed to promote inclusion of neurodiverse or perhaps even more traditionally diverse voices. What we see in a traditional classroom can be a power imbalance rather than a welcoming space. For example, consider a commonly used activity called the "Great Game of Power."[26] In this activity, participants are given four chairs and a water bottle, and one volunteer is asked to silently arrange the objects in a way that gives one of the chairs a position of power. Nothing is allowed to be removed from the activity, but the volunteer is allowed to move the objects in any which way they would like, including placing them on top of one another. The volunteer then returns to their space without sharing what their rationale was behind the arrangement. Sometimes there are a few rounds of this, asking more volunteers to make changes to the arrangement again to make the primary chair more powerful. At the end of the activity, the group at large (minus the volunteers that participated in moving the objects) are asked to interpret the final position of the chairs and water bottle. Oftentimes, especially with multiple rounds of modification, the most powerful chair winds up facing the others, and perhaps they are at this point even flipped over and the most powerful chair is atop a nearby desk or something looking down on the dismantled chairs. Why do we bring up this example? Strangely, it's very typical that the final arrangement of these chairs looks a whole lot like the traditional classroom setup that we see with our professor at the front, sometimes on a raised platform, speaking down to the students who remain in a much lower physical and social level of power.

Undergraduate institutions are currently doing a lot of work to build inclusive classrooms as, again, we are recognizing both multiple forms of intelligence and multiple forms of learning in our college-aged students. Creating an inclusive classroom involves developing an environment where all students, regardless of their background, abilities, or learning styles, feel valued, supported, and able to succeed. This begins with creating an atmosphere where students feel they can express themselves. Language is more important than ever, as we pointed out in our 2020 book *Diversity at College: Real Stories of Students Conquering Bias and Making Higher Education More Inclusive*.[27] With the various identities students hold in the classroom, some of which are concealed, stigmatized identities that students do not display, it is important to avoid assumptions, use language that is inclusive and respectful, remain positive, encourage open communication, and make it clear from the first day of class that all voices are equal and need to be heard.

Universal Design for Learning[28] is a framework emerging in the education system, including at the college level, that aims to make learning accessible and effective for all students regardless of their individual learning styles, abilities, or backgrounds. It is based on the idea that there is no one-size-fits-all approach to education. Instead, it encourages teachers to design curricula that offer multiple means of engagement, representation, and expression. This approach helps create flexible learning environments that accommodate diverse learners and focus on the "why," "what," and "how" of learning. In regard to the why, Universal Design for Learning emphasizes the importance of engaging students by offering various ways to capture their interest and motivation. This might include providing choices in activities, relating content to students' personal interests, and using strategies that promote persistence and self-regulation.

Universal Design for Learning also focuses on providing a variety of classroom activities such as collaborative projects, hands-on experiments, and/or interactive games. In regard to the what, Universal Design for Learning advocates for presenting information in a variety of formats to accommodate different learning preferences. For example, teachers might use text, audio, video, visuals, and hands-on materials all to convey the same content. Content must be accessible, thereby emphasizing the need for materials that all students can use regardless of physical or cognitive abilities. In regard to how, Universal Design for Learning encourages giving students multiple ways to express what they have learned. Instead of relying solely on traditional assessments like written tests, teachers can offer options like oral presentations, creative projects, or digital media. It also supports the development of executive functions (such as goal setting, planning, and time management) and is inclusive of adaptive tools and technologies (such as speech-to-text software and alternative keyboards) to make sure that all students are fully able to participate in and engage with the course.

This is just one framework among many for building inclusive classrooms. All of this begins with creating a space and then getting to know your students. As we mentioned before with the ivory tower of higher education, this is not an easy feat and can oftentimes be put on the back burner when a college professor is under intense deadlines and obligations with research productivity and service in other forms to the institution. With that, though, we do see our colleges and universities creating diversity statements and committing increasingly large budgets to work in this space, providing training on best practices, hiring culturally competent faculty and staff, and bringing faces into higher education that better represent the student population in which we are working. This is important because embracing diversity not only benefits diverse individuals but also enriches society as a whole by fostering creativity, innovation, and a deeper appreciation of the full spectrum of human potential. However, this is just the beginning of work in this sphere, and much institutional and individual commitment is needed to save space for diverse voices in the conversation.

## Cultivating Professional Wisdom in a Diverse Audience

The questions remain. What is intelligence? How do we create it in our undergraduate learners? Additionally, how can we use this to cultivate professional wisdom—the theme of this book? We believe that intelligence comes in various forms, and in our opinion professional wisdom results from a cultivation of multiple intelligences. If we take Gardner's approach and focus on the multiple types of intelligence, it seems sensible that professional wisdom would blend the sort of academic intelligence that is more logical, mathematic, and linguistic that we see in our scientists, engineers, journalists, and lawyers with that spatial, bodily, kinesthetic intelligence that we see in our tradespeople. In an internship experience where we really believe someone nurtures the development of this professional wisdom, one would also be tending to their interpersonal and intrapersonal intelligence as well, as the social and self-awareness aspects of this concept are equally as important. Remember when we said that the Northeastern students left for their internship at age nineteen or twenty but returned at age twenty-six (figuratively, of course, because they were only gone for a semester or two)? That is what we are talking about. Maturation of all of these different forms of intelligence is necessary for the development of professional wisdom.

With our diverse undergraduate learners, there is no one straightforward answer to what should be done in the classroom and what should be required or encouraged as experiential learning opportunities. But by embracing the unique strengths and needs of each student, using flexible teaching methods, and fostering a supportive and welcoming environment, we can help all students succeed and feel valued in our classrooms. This approach not only benefits diverse students but also enriches the learning experience for everyone, promoting a culture of respect, empathy, and collaboration. Training internship coordinators who can not only work with companies that are aware of the need for diversity in the workforce but can also work with diverse individuals and know best practices in the space is also going to be key to creating professional wisdom in our college graduates.

Understanding that every student is unique is also a key piece of this equation. Simply because a student does not excel in an economics course does not mean that they lack the intelligence necessary to develop professional wisdom in the field of business. On the flip side of that, just because a student excels in the lab during an undergraduate research course with pipetting skills beyond any of their labmates also does not mean that they are professionally wise. Remember, we believe that learning through experience is a brain-natural phenomena driven by likes and dislikes from an experience itself. Developing a professional skill that complements an A from a course seems like a recipe for professional wisdom. Without the implicit circuits of the brain telling the student that they actually like what they are doing, and without the cognitive reflection on that experience, our students will not become professionally wise. In order to truly help them develop this ability, the equation must be unique for every individual. The only thing we know for sure is that professional wisdom increases employability. Challenging our students to take that internship, shadow that doctor, work in that business office for the summer, and so on are the best ways we can create intelligence that is wise and tap into that implicit and explicit brain while tying all of these elements together.

## Summary

Intelligence comes in various forms. We see this in our college-aged students as they excel in specific courses and topics and shy away from or struggle with others. This is partially due to the implicit circuits of the brain telling the student whether they "like" or "dislike" the course or topic, but it is also strongly influenced by the modality in which the course is taught. All students tend to have different learning styles, or ways in which they learn best. For some of us this shows itself through listening to a lecture, whereas for others it is through visualizations such as flowcharts and concept maps. Educators must keep this in mind when developing academic courses, as it is extremely important to engage all learners in the classroom. Now more than ever we are recognizing the value of voices from all learners, especially first-generation students (those who are first in their family to attend college), students of color, students with lower socioeconomic status, neurodiverse students, and many other underrepresented groups. Creating inclusive classrooms is a challenge, but we believe that it is an essential element for colleges and universities, especially in cultivating this special form of intelligence that we refer to as professional knowledge.

Chapter 8

# Impacts of COVID-19 and Remote Learning on Professional Wisdom

There are events in the lives of all students that they remember. For our older readers, perhaps that was what they were doing the day that JFK was assassinated. For our millennials, perhaps it is which class they were in when they heard of the 9/11 attacks. This is how Generation Z will view the COVID-19 pandemic. They will forever be able to tell us what grade they were in, what changes were made, and their initial excitement that shifted to a longing to go back to in-person learning. They will remember their own struggles with technology and access to resources such as computers, cameras, and high-speed internet, as well as struggles with how to navigate Zoom and the online learning environment. They will remember us teachers struggling to put students in breakout rooms, talking with the microphone on mute and not noticing, not activating online assignments, and doing our best to create inclusive virtual classrooms while maintaining integrity. It was no easy feat for any of us, as students or professors.

The COVID-19 pandemic really began in higher education in the second half of the winter term of 2020, as classes settled into a month or more of remote teaching that spring term and lasted four academic terms, into the fall of 2021.[1] In addition to the disease itself that eventually killed more than a million Americans and cost the economy some $13 trillion,[2] the move to remote learning forced all of the faculty and students not already doing online remote education to figure out how to figure things out—and to do so as fast as possible with limited, if any, training. It is true that on a program like Zoom, Webex, Teams, or Google Meet, one can see the teacher and the other students, but the little boxes were no match for most people compared with the full personal presence of being together in the real world. For our college students, they had to forget about internships in the workplace unless they were also online. Through the pandemic, people disconnected, and the application of direct experience to academic learning was largely suspended, especially for most experiential applications. Without this real-world and emotional impact on the cognitive-emotional integration of a college education, we figure that the formation of practical wisdom in college largely stalled.

## The Academic and Professional Cost of COVID-19

The COVID-19 pandemic has had a significant impact on education, leading to widespread learning loss among high school and college students. This learning loss is a result of multiple factors, including school closures, the shift to remote learning, and the emotional and psychological effects of the pandemic on students. Recent studies have attempted to quantify this learning loss, and generally, across all locations worldwide and in all subject areas, significant deficits were reported.[3] Some individual studies find differences in various aspects of learning loss, such as one that reported different amounts at different ages in different subjects (specifically math),[4] but nonetheless the phenomena is undeniable. Another important part of this phenomenon is the significantly higher learning loss that we see in disadvantaged student populations across the country. Losses are over 10 percent higher in populations that did not have equitable resources to other students and communities.[5]

While there is not much data yet about the specific impacts of COVID-19 on the undergraduate student's learning loss and the impact this will have on employability, we know learning loss was a result of numerous variables during the COVID-19 pandemic, starting with disruption to learning environments.

Many students were unprepared for the sudden transition from in-person to remote learning. Access to technology and stable internet connections was inconsistent, leading to gaps in learning. Also, the lack of face-to-face interaction with teachers and peers hindered the ability to grasp complex concepts, particularly in subjects like math and science.[6,7] There was also a large variation in remote learning quality. As our students would agree, not all remote learning experiences were equal. Some students had access to well-structured online curricula, while others faced poorly organized or less engaging content. Again, this digital divide disproportionately affected students from low-income families, contributing to greater learning loss in underserved communities. We also saw a large emotional and psychological impact, as the pandemic increased anxiety, stress, and depression among students. These mental health challenges affected their ability to focus, engage, and perform academically. The lack of social interaction, difficulty communicating with a digital face on a screen, and reduced opportunity for extracurricular activities also impacted students' overall well-being and motivation to learn. Additionally, especially in the first semester of the pandemic, there was a loss of instructional time, either because of shortened school days or fewer days of instruction.

As professors, we have spent a lot of time in department meetings discussing the impacts of COVID-19 on our incoming freshmen, as there is an evident lack of preparedness for higher education. In a recent study of high school juniors, only 18 percent of them reported being prepared to enter college,[8] and we see this firsthand. Changes have been made to our freshmen curricula to meet students where they are at. This makes it difficult to fit the material from pre-COVID times into the first semester. Many high schools adapted graduation requirements because of issues in students being able to hit them all. The cancellation or modification of standardized tests (e.g., SAT, ACT, Regents Exams in New York State) during the switch to online learning disrupted the college admissions process. Many schools removed the requirement for standardized testing during this time because students simply did not have access to it.

Colleges and universities were forced to respond to this with little information. *The Chronicle of Higher Education* released a report titled *The Future of Gen Z: How COVID-19 Will Shape Students and Higher Education for the Next Decade*,[9] in which they discuss some interesting points on how students and parents are now expecting more from colleges, inside and outside of the classroom. This partially has to do with the fact that many do not agree that the online education many students were experiencing during the pandemic was worth the tuition paid. One survey of more than three thousand US and Canadian students reported that nearly 80 percent of students stated their online courses lacked the engagement of in-person classes.[10] As colleges responded to this by implementing things such as small tuition reductions, it almost enforced the idea that the quality of a remote classroom experience was less than the traditional in-class experience. As students returned to the classroom, they were coming from a time of immediate response (one-click ordering and information readily at hand on devices), and assistance from AI soon emerged. Colleges struggled to keep up with these demands and make the speed of their customer experience, or student experience, on par with what students and parents have come to expect during the pandemic. Budgetary constraints are one cause of this, especially with COVID-19–related cuts to positions; one must also consider the difficulties posed by the fact that offices such as admissions, the registrar, and financial aid are being used more than ever. There is a similar strain on faculty members, as the pandemic has created more need from the students, so often our office hours extend far beyond the assigned times, and we are backed up on emails from previous days that we have not had the time to get to.

In regard to the impact of COVID-19 on our college students, they specifically faced challenges adapting to fully online or hybrid learning models. Courses that require hands-on learning, such as labs or clinicals, were particularly affected. While science professors did their best to offer virtual laboratory options, it is just not the same to be asked about the distal end of the humerus on a two-dimensional image when, if the student were in lab, they would have their hands on a skeleton identifying this bone marking by feel. Many students reported a decline in the quality of education, with concerns about the value of their degrees. Additionally, the American Association of Collegiate Registrars and Admissions Officers reported a significant impact on academics: The shift to remote learning led to an increase in incomplete grades, withdrawals, and academic probation cases.[11] Also, out of the 622 colleges interviewed in their data set, 73 percent of them reported making significant changes to the grading and transcript practices in response to the COVID-19 pandemic. We saw changes to pass/fail policies, transfer credits, and withdrawal deadlines, as well as much stronger suggestions toward singling out COVID-19 grades as a unique set of scores that stand in their own place in an academic portfolio. Furthermore, disruption to internships, research opportunities, and other experiential learning affected students' career preparation and the ability of the college to count these experiences as credit-bearing activities. In programs such as nursing (which requires a specific number of hours of hands-on clinical experience) or physician assistant studies (which requires approximately twelve hundred hours of clinical time just to apply), colleges, universities, and the students themselves were put to the ultimate test to get creative and hit these suddenly extremely challenging standards to achieve. Again, this put our undergraduate institutions in a difficult place, as increasing pressure was coming in from parents and students regarding this unexpected need.

COVID-19 also came with a huge professional cost. Just to mention a few instances, the initial waves of the pandemic led to widespread layoffs and furloughs, particularly in industries such as hospitality, retail, travel, and entertainment. Millions of workers globally lost their jobs as businesses struggled to stay afloat, with disproportionate rates of these individuals being from minority backgrounds. Even for those who retained their jobs, many experienced pay cuts, reduced hours, or lost bonuses and incentives. This led to increased financial insecurity and difficulties in managing personal and family finances. Taking this back to our college students, the US Census Bureau's Household Pulse Survey from August through December of 2020 reported that 75 percent of households with a college-aged student adapted their plans to accommodate changes to their family unit brought on by the pandemic.[12] Over a third of these households reported putting their student's education plan on hold at that time for reasons including a need for that student to serve as a caretaker in the household or to work a job and supplement the income for the family. Other reasons included changes to their financial aid package, being unable to afford the tuition, and changes to their expectations of college, including living arrangements or classroom settings (whether in person or virtual).

For students and professionals in training, the pandemic disrupted education and professional development opportunities. Many internships, apprenticeships, and hands-on training programs were postponed or canceled, affecting future career prospects. Professional development programs and continuing education shifted online, which, while accessible, also posed challenges related to engagement, quality, and the effectiveness of virtual learning. Researchers are now beginning to report on the loss of skill and productivity that the professional sector has also seen as a result of COVID-19 unemployment and a lack of new job creation.[13] As workers lose skills during periods of unemployment, as college students are unable to learn skills because of remote challenges, and as the labor force deteriorates, we are faced with a huge challenge—especially in higher education—to find creative solutions.

## Other Challenges to the Classroom and Professional Wisdom

Overlapping with challenges emerging during the COVID-19 pandemic came challenges from the advancement of AI. Gen Z has been surrounded by digital technology their entire lives. They are comfortable using smartphones, social media, and the internet for communication, entertainment, and education. This familiarity with technology means they often expect seamless, intuitive digital experiences in all aspects of life, including education. The internet provides

Generation Z with unparalleled access to information. They can learn about almost any topic through online resources like YouTube, Wikipedia, and educational platforms such as Khan Academy or Coursera. Educational technology offers personalized learning experiences, allowing students to learn at their own pace and according to their preferred learning style. Adaptive learning platforms and apps tailor content to individual needs. With all of this, students and parents begin to question what the need is for higher education and the traditional practices we currently see in academia.

We as academics have had to pivot as a response to these changing student expectations. As this generation tends to prefer video content and interactive media over traditional text-based resources, we have shifted the ways in which we present information. Growing up with constant access to information and entertainment has also contributed to shorter attention spans. Generation Z is skilled at multitasking and often juggles multiple screens and tasks simultaneously, which requires teaching methods that are dynamic, concise, and varied to maintain engagement. Social media has made Generation Z highly connected, and they often prefer collaborative learning environments where they can share ideas and work together, both online and in-person. Embedding and requiring the use of platforms such as the Google suite (Sheets, Docs, Slides, etc.) are ways to reach and engage our students. This generation values personalized learning experiences that cater to their individual interests and needs. They appreciate educational technologies that allow them to learn at their own pace and on their own terms. Adaptive learning platforms, personalized feedback, and flexible course options (such as online or hybrid courses for the learners specifically seeking them) are increasingly important in meeting their expectations of higher education. Surprisingly, over ten million US students were taking at least one college course online during the fall of 2022 despite higher education returning to an in-person format by this time.[14] Compared with before the pandemic, this is approximately 2.85 million more students taking at least one course online, with relatively similar numbers of students attending college. With this online learning being the new norm, it is undoubtable that this comes at a cost to the development of professional wisdom.

As Generation Z (and Generation Alpha that follows it) continues to shape the landscape of higher education, institutions are likely to invest more in technology that supports personalized, flexible, and interactive learning experiences. The role of educators will also evolve, with a greater focus on guiding students in how to effectively use technology for learning, critically evaluate information, and develop digital literacy skills. The integration of emerging technologies like AI could further transform the educational experience, making it more tailored to the needs and preferences of Generation Z/Alpha. With that and the release of ChatGPT in November of 2022, though, comes its own set of challenges and benefits. We will touch on some of those in the next chapter.

## Professional Wisdom Development Was Damaged by the COVID-19 Pandemic

Professional wisdom depends upon the appraisal that the student makes of their success or failure in the contextually rich world of direct experience, something that was made extremely challenging during the COVID-19 pandemic. It is the previously discussed thin slicing of Malcolm Gladwell[15] or the operation of system 1 by Daniel Kahneman.[16] These gut-level judgments have a value component to them that operates in the limbic system. The second piece of this puzzle is that humans are built to read each other's faces and body language as part of our social interactions. These sometimes unconscious signals transmit impressions and feelings between us, and they can be invaluable in forming an evaluation of the intellectual content. This connection between people in psychology is sometimes called "theory of mind,"[17] and it really involves a kind of mind reading based on the physical interaction between people. This is something that we get in the classroom or an internship but is again something really challenging on a computer monitor in remote learning.

An excellent example of how we may read each other comes from neuroscience. It is the story of the well-known mirror neurons that become active in your motor system whenever an action that you could do is done by someone else. It is thought that the logic of executing a command to move from the motor parts of your brain is used by the perception parts of your brain to understand what it is that the other wants to do.[18] Notice the emphasis on "wants." These neurons appear to react to what the movement is designed to accomplish, like picking up a bit of food and eating it.

These mirror neurons also pick up on emotion, which even from a very young age is critical for communication. Babies are able to mimic facial expressions, such as smiling or sticking out their tongues, which is believed to be facilitated by mirror neurons. Mirror neurons also help babies understand the intentions behind actions. For example, when a baby sees someone reaching for an object, mirror neurons may help the baby grasp the intention of reaching for that object, even before they can do it themselves (back to those wants). These neurons are also likely involved in the development of empathy. As babies observe the emotions of others, mirror neurons help them "mirror" those emotions, contributing to emotional bonding and social learning. These neurons continue to actively and more efficiently work as we age and continue to learn from what we are seeing others do.

While the purely cognitive flow of information is pretty good in remote learning (if the technology is good and the teaching is good), remote learning can be like reading. It is an exchange of explicit information. It is like you got the recipe for making a blueberry pie, for which we are sure you can find thousands of recipes within seconds using the internet. As mentioned earlier, it is not surprising that after one makes ten or twenty blueberry pies, that experience leads to a deeper understanding of the enterprise and, thus, a better pie.

Unfortunately, the emotional flow is impaired with remote learning. Without both kinds of input and their interaction, it is sometimes said that cognitive learning alone is like "rowing a boat with one oar," at least in terms of developing implicit as well as explicit understanding. It is harder to make forward progress in that boat, and it is harder to grow in the development of professional wisdom. Already college is too safe and predictable of an environment for such full development. And that is why many students find being on a jobsite or studying abroad or interacting directly with a professor on their research to be so different from sitting in class. It is the possibility of success and indeed of failure that teaches a student how the ideas work in practice and gives them the feel for what works in a field, and that is practical wisdom (skill-based wisdom).

Of course, the danger of remote learning is that it is tempting to sit back and watch the presentation rather than engage, absorbing the facts passively like you were watching a documentary. While auditory learners might excel at this and even watch the lecture a few times to get the information to fully sink in, a course should not simply be this alone. Courses have assessments and exams to test for knowledge gained, which offer feedback and sometimes show failure points to the student. These could be learning moments, even if they are designed for grading purposes. Essay exams or tests with some kind of generated knowledge display are better than just recognizing the right answer in a list as in multiple-choice tests. They are more natural to the real world (few people ask each other multiple-choice questions) and they provide opportunities for failure. Even when the essay exam is a success and the student gets a good grade, the possibility of failure is still there. Courses also have interaction: Whether this comes from a discussion, a professor calling on student volunteers or otherwise, group projects or breakout rooms (especially if virtual), there is a social component that must be hit in this virtual world. Additionally, remembering to appeal to the diverse audience and create an inclusive space for not only the multiple learning styles of our students but also the multiple underrepresented identities in the classroom is critical and a challenge in the virtual environment.

## How Can We Fight Back Against This Effect of Remote Learning and Technology?

The answer involves engagement and even the prospect of failure. Some feel that doing, trying, succeeding, and failing builds practical wisdom, as Barry Schwartz has spoken about (and as mentioned in his book with Kenneth Sharpe, this goes back to Aristotle).[19] The application of practical wisdom to professional wisdom is clear. As discussed in Schwartz's TED Talk, craftspeople back in the time of Aristotle found a way to make a flexible ruler (not a stick) so they could easily measure the circumference of a column they were building. In a sense, he says, this is "bending the rule." But it is really to get to the goal—what Aristotle calls "telos," or purpose.

It is what a skilled mason feels and sees when they are adding water to a large container of mortar ingredients. There is a perfect consistency to that mortar that the mason knows. If a homeowner trying to save a few dollars were to be reading an instruction manual and it said, "not too wet and not too dry for the best results," they would have no idea how to discern the right consistency. Take baking: If the recipe said, "Do not overbeat," the amateur cook in the kitchen might spin their spoon in the bowl ten times when really the best results needed fifty spins. Our experienced mason and baker, though, they just know. Not only can they do it themselves; they can look at another's finished product and intrinsically feel exactly what went wrong. Of course, this book is not about masonry or baking but making decisions in life using this idea of feeling (at an unconscious gut level) versus just pure, calculating, cognitive intellect. You need both practical wisdom as well as the passion and feel for the profession to truly create professional wisdom.

It is a challenge for colleges to accomplish this fostering of knowledge and skill, especially in an online environment. In addition to online courses, we are seeing an increasing number of hybrid and other types of courses where the instructor comes to the student as a box on a computer screen (on the online platform of choice) if there is a face-to-face component, or if the course is designed as a fully asynchronous course, then the instructor and the student never actually meet. We think one way is to provide for real work, perhaps with other students, that has the potential to fail or succeed.

In our classes where we use Zoom meetings in a hybrid format, we employ group work. This can be tricky if the instructor is not present to observe interactions in the Zoom room. Nevertheless, the need for the students to produce a product, perhaps to report back to the whole class in that session, gives at least some people in the group a chance to succeed or fail. There is even the possibility that some students may thrive in this more occluded environment and blossom. For others, the act of speaking to each other and trying to appear knowledgeable and intelligent could be a factor. It is true that some may just sit and observe, but that is also true in many in-person classes, particularly if they are in a large lecture hall with hundreds of seats. The point is to get the students to put some of their feelings, judgment, and implicit thinking on the line for other group members (and maybe eventually the instructor) to evaluate. The prospect of failure, so managed, makes it more real than just watching the instructor like a television show and then getting tested on the topic later.

Zoom and similar platforms are handy tools, and there are elements to them that keep the students engaged and provide instant feedback. Use of live polls and quizzes with tools like Mentimeter, Kahoot!, or the built-in features of any video conferencing platform can assist in creating interaction. Breakout rooms of course help with collaboration, and enriching them with a facilitator such as a teaching assistant deepens conversations. Digital whiteboards like Jamboard, Miro, or any whiteboard feature in a video conferencing tool allows students to collaborate on visual tasks or brainstorm ideas in real time. Participation can also be encouraged through the chat feature for quick questions and comments. Discussion boards can be used for more in-depth conversations and peer interaction between classes. Group projects—especially long-term group projects that require collaboration over several weeks and encourage the use of tools like Google Docs, Trello, or Slack for students to manage their work and communicate—also help the virtual environment. Peer review further encourages critical thinking and collaborative learning. As professors, we have seen vastly different levels of faculty engagement in online courses, and there is no one right answer. These suggestions that we provide are elements that we have found successful and that others agree are best practices in online learning. Creating interactive virtual classes requires careful planning, the right tools, and a focus on engaging students through varied, dynamic activities. Bringing a human element to a virtual course is a challenge, but a student cannot begin to develop professional wisdom without interaction with others. Interpersonal intelligence and the ability to respond to feedback, whether it be in regard to a success or failure, is critical.

Since the pandemic is over and many organizations (especially universities) have moved back to much more in-person operation, remote learning now has to adapt to that environment. The "threat" of an in-person encounter has grown in teaching and could be very useful in designing assignments, making practice sessions, and focusing a bit beyond the course content itself to its application. We instructors could use remote learning components as convenient information transmission situations, like having the students also read a book. But at some point, there has to be person-to-person interaction. Here might be where some professional wisdom learning could creep in for instructors, particularly if there is a practitioner in the classroom (or Zoom room).

Professors have a responsibility to find ways to get students engaged, put "skin in the game" of production, and then help them improve their practice and maybe develop some marketable skills. Remote learning is not a hindrance to this engagement activity, but it requires something from the instructor to promote the engagement. We recommend to anyone asked to create online courses to find a mentor who is experienced, more knowledgeable, and in authority over the course. Perhaps they have taught the course before or something similar. They have a gravity about them to the younger students that can be an important source of encouragement if deployed properly. It can also be a brutal put-down and discouraging if deployed improperly. While this mentoring can be done remotely and may be the only way it can operate in some classes, it is naturally stronger if the instructor and student are present together in the real world, where the contextual interaction is its richest. While we could debate the value of an in-person education versus an online education for days, our point here is that for professional wisdom, engagement is necessary, and we are both glad to be back in the classroom face-to-face with our students.

## Summary

COVID-19 was an extremely challenging time for individuals as well as for the entire educational system. To accommodate learning, there was an undeniably necessary shift to an online environment that attempted to create inclusive spaces while students were all secluded in their homes and small family units. With that, we must recognize that remote learning is not bad in itself, but it can be if it separates the implicit learning or emotional transmission of what was valuable in the information between the student and the teacher. That can happen today, post–COVID-19, but it does not have to. Some courses online and some video examples of good, value-laden teaching of content exist. We instructors even use them in our in-person classes as supplements, like another instructor that the students can see anytime. The trick here is to have a connection with the students, not just let them figure it out on their own with your good but heartless framework that transmits knowledge but does little for the early development of professional wisdom.

Chapter 9

# The Future of Higher Education in Combining Skills with Knowledge:
## Technology, AI, and Government

Jim has lived through a few technical challenges. Perhaps most notable was the first appearance of the internet in the early 1980s, which connected us all and put knowledge in the hands of everyone, not just the professors. Of course, that knowledge was sometimes uncritical, at least compared with the curation of that knowledge by professors in classes and through books by reputable companies. But the next step was even more dramatic: the introduction of powerful portable devices (such as today's cell phones, laptops, iPads, etc.) that students could easily bring to classes. This made knowledge even more accessible, allowing students to look up material in the classroom while the professors were talking. On college campuses, the library of the world is literally at a student's fingertips, especially with search engines. As teachers, both of your coauthors enjoyed this development, as it allowed us to focus our teaching more on critical concepts while students could check the facts that underlie that critical thinking. We even found ourselves learning tricks for navigating this world from our students.

To us, the next step has just arrived, and it is AI. AI has taken some impressive steps—especially in the last few years—and like other industries, higher education is reacting in many ways. While some have argued that the presence of AI calls for a more important focus on what is learned in experiential education,[1] a topic to which we will return in the last chapter, one clearly already appreciated downside is the potential for student cheating. Students can now easily go beyond looking up facts and ideas when writing assigned papers. In take-home essay tests, students can simply ask something like ChatGPT to write it for them. The response is fast enough to fit into the allocated take-home exam time parameters. While websites and programs currently exist for instructors to look for internet copy-and-paste-type cheating, new AI makes it more complicated because the AI-generated text is original. AI-checking websites do exist and can indicate a student's potential use of ChatGPT, but these sites are not 100 percent accurate, and so one cannot accuse a student of cheating like one could back in the recent old days when the checking programs showed instructors the exact website to compare with the student's submitted text. An exact copy was proof enough.

So, what to do? Jim still gives at-home, open-book essay tests. When an answer seems funny to the reader (professor or TA), we run it through an AI detection website, which gives a guesstimate of how much was written by AI versus written by a human. Then, the professor calls the student before the grade is posted. Face-to-face (on Zoom or in person), we discuss the answer. If the student clearly knows nothing of the subject matter, a conversation about cheating then can ensue. If they do know the answer, then the story gets more complicated, and it is harder to prove the student cheated. Also, back to that ivory tower of education: With classes of sometimes over one hundred students, this can be extremely time consuming for a professor. But it is also a lesson in how to use AI (or any internet lookup) without pirating words. We keep saying in the syllabus and in the instructions on the essay exams that we want to see "your words, your thinking" in these essay test responses. The alternative is to give in-class paper exams, like the old days. But that does seem like it is going a bit backward, even if it may sometimes be necessary.

Our challenge now in the higher education classroom is to figure out how to use AI with the students to drive their understanding of concepts, not circumvent it, so as to contribute to the development of critical thinking and professional wisdom. As discussed previously, it is a bit like the challenge with remote learning, but it is even harder now. This pushes us as professors and administrators to use our critical-thinking skills to integrate this technology into the classroom rather than put our efforts into banning it. Outside of the classroom, too, we must realize the potential of AI in that it can accomplish amazing feats, such as creating personally tuned college application lists for future students. Perhaps those lists will have a focus on institutions where the contribution of professional development is a significant part of the degree program. This is us speaking as former administrators or for administrators, so let us discuss.

## The Role of Technology in Choosing a College

AI allows for this new challenge to higher education enrollment, reputation, and basic marketing. Unfortunately for some institutions, declining enrollments in a time of budget challenges is causing them to close their doors even after a hundred years or more of existence. Across this nation, we saw the closure of forty-eight colleges in 2022 and another thirty in the first half of 2023.[2] More closed in 2024 when we were writing this book. This trend just keeps continuing, and it's not because of corruption or misappropriation of funds. It may be because the colleges still cannot bounce back from some enrollment declines following the pandemic. Or it may be due to a demographic decline in college-aged students. However, we think that the presumption of the market is that such institutions are no longer attractive enough to students and their families, given the required price and time commitment. What students want and have always wanted is an education that is not only engaging and inspiring but also helps them grow professionally, whether they are headed into further education or directly into a career path after graduation. If they cannot see that in a college experience and they can in other institutions, one can guess where they will apply.

AI has the potential to combine the information from student transcripts with students' personal interests to help them figure out which colleges to apply to for admission. That is, we think that AI will likely soon provide a highly individual (personalized) ranking of colleges and universities based on data about the schools and the characteristics and expectations of individual student applicants. In the old days, this was done by knowledgeable guidance counselors—human intelligence—who met with the student, discussed their interests and ambitions as well as their high school records, and recommended colleges or universities that were a good fit. Now, we have AI technology that will save the student not only time but also some fees associated with the application process.

Again, we predict that one of the key components of that student choice in that future ranking system will be the ability of the school to educate the student into an employment or into a postgraduate education outcome. To do well in those future rankings, the school will depend not only on excellent intellectual training the students get from the classes taught by caring professors but also on what key skills and abilities the students will gain from internships and other forms of direct (perhaps workplace) experiences, and how those help them enter a career or go on for further education in a particular field.

The idea is that the choice of a college education could be personalized in an AI-developed ranking based on the applicant's characteristics and interests. AI will take into account the current higher education institutional characteristics that go into a college's or university's ranking, such as the profile of its faculty and the nature of its facilities and programs. But it could also take into account an institution's record of success in the student's chosen field. That could start with the student's interest at the time, but AI may even take into account fields to which that student may likely switch (e.g., premed to public health) if they change their mind.

The AI ranking of the future is likely to also incorporate postgraduate employment outcomes from labor department databases and the institution's history. That kind of a ranking will come as yet another core challenge to universities. Now they will be compelled to do something to help students get experiences that will lead to postgraduate success. Perhaps there will be more pressure to do what the cooperative education schools already do in helping students get paid workplace experiences to complement their academic education while in college, as we previously discussed.

These higher education institutions of the future will need to do personal career development within their institutional financial means. We are sure they will have technology that will likely not look quite like the experiential programs started long ago by cooperative education schools that are now built into an institution's processes and budgets. They will achieve the same purpose of putting the student in jobs and internships in these fields. Ironically, the same AI technology that we think will drive this personalized ranking can also help schools put their best foot forward in these future personalized rankings with whatever populations of students the college or university wants to target—ideally, the "fit."

## Studying Higher Education and Employment

As a response to this, we do see the development of centers in and out of universities that study this employability issue, and we take their existence as further evidence for the growing trend driven by market forces. Let's just consider a few centers here as examples. Georgetown University is home to the Center on Education and the Workforce.[3] It just issued a 2024 report called "The Great Misalignment,"[4] which discusses middle skills that often drive employment in the trades and other similar professions. The report points out the mismatch between what is taught in and out of community college and what is needed in the local market. It offers some interesting observations, one of which is that this mismatch is stronger in rural areas than in urban areas. Another example is the Center for Workforce Innovation and Solutions, a division of the W. E. Upjohn Institute for Employment Research,[5] a private, non-profit operation with a long history in the state of Michigan. A third example is Rutgers University's Education and Employment Research Center. Of course, research centers exist at America's three oldest cooperative education universities (Cincinnati,[6] Northeastern,[7] and Drexel[8]), as well as in many other forward-thinking institutions such as Elon University.[9] We could write a book about just the cooperative education aspect of the higher education industry, and work done inside and outside of higher education institutions, that support simple employability.

## Partnerships from Technology-Driven Companies

Colleges and universities do not have to just work on their own to figure out how to prepare students to learn from the workforce. They can partner with companies whose products leverage technology to help students gain these experiences. There is precedent for this in another industry: biotechnology. In Boston in particular (Jim is speaking from the experience of living through this), larger firms do not develop all the biologicals in their profile of pending drugs. Sometimes the larger companies watch small biotech companies develop a product through the discovery stage and then buy them to incorporate that discovery into their own business. We are not suggesting that universities buy AI or other such technology companies that are focused on helping students develop important experiences so they can grow professionally while in college. But they could partner with them. We will discuss a few examples here, but the reader should know that this field is rapidly changing, so these are simply a few present examples. Also, the discussion here of these companies is not meant to endorse them but merely to illustrate the possibilities for future interaction with the higher education industry that higher education ignores at its peril.

Looking to find an internship in college? Try Handshake, a company formed in 2014 by a college student from Michigan Tech who was looking for a way to expand the ability of college students to access internships and is now in thousands of colleges and universities, including more than 90 percent of the top universities.[10] Handshake connects students with workplace internships, something LinkedIn[11] or Indeed[12] or ZipRecruiter[13] already does for everyone, but Handshake focuses on college students. It also helps colleges and universities provide better career services.

While those career services operations also recommend students develop a LinkedIn profile or use other software, they actually use Handshake to connect students with internship possibilities. Career services always did that, but through their own connections (especially with alumni, as keeping it within the "family" is very effective). They also use job fairs, where companies come to campus to recruit graduating students but also to look for interns, perhaps as future employees after graduation. Handshake allows such connections to be made online at any time and at a cost that is affordable compared with hiring more staff for career services to find and make those employer connections themselves. As of this writing, Handshake states it has fifteen million students at more than fifteen hundred colleges and universities with more than nine hundred employers on the system.[14]

Need to practice your first job talk? InStage is a young company out of Canada that has an online virtual reality package where students can practice what may be their first internship interview by talking to online avatars.[15] Through the use of AI, the avatars respond back like a job interviewer. To date, students held such conversations with career services people or with friends and colleagues, or perhaps they practiced their interviewing skills in the mirror. Here, the avatars provide realistic online interviews, giving a student a safe way to confidentially prepare for job interviews. And they can do it anytime, anywhere. More recently, they have even developed an avatar-based way to do reflection while the student is on a cooperative education experience.

In terms of actual content, the AI system also incorporates the student's uploaded resume and the particular job/internship description before the mock interview starts. While one can always just record a practice interview on one's phone and maybe even send the video to a career services person for a critique, here the feedback is immediate, confidential, and comes with some statistics like average speaking rate compared with norms or use of filler words because it comes from AI-powered avatars. There are even other options for this kind of avatar technology that are currently being explored by Jim in the classroom by adapting this job interview format to provide a speaking modality for students to answer quiz questions by speaking, not just by writing.[16] Our hope is that it promotes active learning in a standard class. Of course, as AI spreads, universities are employing their own programs such as Big Interview at Northeastern University,[17] but even this cooperative education school is, reportedly, working with InStage, as is Waterloo University, another major cooperative education school.

There are many such applications for higher education within and outside of the world of experiential education. For example, Khan Academy is working on a way to turn ChatGPT into a mentor that could scale economically to help students find the answer and not just give it to them.[18]

Interested in developing your skills to make yourself more marketable after college? iQ4 is a cybersecurity training company that features a digital repository or e-portfolio of job skills the student has developed or might develop, called a wallet.[19] It also uses AI, but to digest skills from a student's resume or even their transcript. It can apply that student skill set to potential jobs and/or show the student what classes or internships might expand the student's skills portfolio to make them more attractive for such a position. iQ4 began in the cybersecurity area, in part because it could work with job skills data from the National Initiative for Cybersecurity Education (NICE).[20] It is expanding to other fields where job skills data using the student's digital wallet is important.

This approach gives the student a sense of what they could do in seeking employment, something that had previously only been available through coaching in the career services office or from other personal sources or by trial and error in job applications after college. For example, Western Governors University has worked with iQ4 to develop the Achievement Wallet, which helps their students plot a career development path.[21]

All of these opportunities aid our students with the development of professional wisdom, but there are emerging tools that make this applied skill development even more possible during the undergraduate experience. iQ4 is unique in that they also facilitate virtual internships and courses that make the development of these skills more accessible. What iQ4 does that makes a difference is that typically an industry mentor (not a faculty member) is in the online Zoom room, and they are typically currently employed in the cybersecurity field. The course (real-world or virtual) often uses a format that is like a capstone course where the students emulate a team that is solving an authentic example of a cybersecurity problem: a case study approach. At the end, the students often present (sometimes in the real world even if the course is virtual) to the mentors and other cyber professionals their team recommends, as though they were a real company. This is then placed in the NICE skills profile, which follows them to actual jobs they might be applying for in the future.

Another AI-based tool being developed is called the digital twin.[22] A digital twin is not a company but a dynamic, real-time virtual counterpart that mirrors the physical state and behavior of its physical counterpart, often using data from LiDAR sensors to continuously update the digital model.[23] LiDAR, or Light Detection and Ranging, is a remote sensing technology that uses laser light to measure distances. It works by emitting laser pulses toward a target and measuring the time it takes for the pulses to bounce back to the sensor. By calculating the time delay, the LiDAR system can determine the distance to the target with high accuracy. Using this information, there is a potentially limitless number of digital twins that technology can create, with these digital twins looking nearly identical to the actual source.

Currently, LiDAR and digital twin technology is used in various spaces.[24] In manufacturing, this technology helps optimize production lines, predict maintenance needs, and improve product designs. In health care, it can model patient-specific treatments or monitor the health of medical devices like pacemakers. In aerospace, driving simulators, and construction and real estate, it can improve design processes, monitor building performance, predict maintenance needs, and allow for testing and optimization in a virtual environment, reducing the need for physical prototypes and trials. Where we see this potentially emerging in colleges is in spaces such as homeland security, where entire infrastructures can be mapped virtually to any location in the world. With this, college students would have the ability to create effective hazard mitigation simulations that can play out digitally in their actual surroundings. Students would be able to access simulations in buildings across the world and test potential plans such as evacuating in response to a disaster.[25] On the flip side, if they had the LiDAR scan of their own building, they could literally take the room they are sitting in and virtually create and assess responses to any sort of threat.

Digital twins and LiDAR can also be used to create city-specific simulations for first responders. A LiDAR map could be created of a specific local concert hall and simulations could be played out for police and firefighters: in response to an armed concertgoer, a fire, a flood, a building collapse, or dozens of other manmade or natural disasters. This could also be used for EMTs and paramedics to treat patients at the digital twin site in response to the disaster. Advances in this technology and increased access could enable our students to get clinical hours on simulations at any hospital in the world that participated in the digital twin platform.

Taking this back to the view of job interviewing, there is a component of professional wisdom that comes from the experience at the jobsite. We discussed information being moved from active learning to habit in the neural circuits, and what if some of this could be circumvented by training in a digital twin? Locating an office, the coffee room, or even the bathroom during the first week of an on-site internship is a challenge. LiDAR and digital twins could enable new interns to tour facilities and gain some basic knowledge about the jobsite prior to even arriving. In regard to virtual interviewing, the entire human resources floor of a specific company could be mapped with this technology, or someone could create a virtual internship building where an intern would have to go through the actual motions of entering the building, checking in with the secretary, and so on, all prior to the interview itself. It could then use avatars and AI to conduct the interview and again offer feedback, as iQ4 is currently doing. The possibilities extend much further than this discussion, and a quick search will turn up companies trying to use it in higher education, but bringing this back to our point: Colleges and universities must be willing to integrate these technologies into their campuses. In regard to professional wisdom, these technologies can help its cultivation in our college students, especially with the current challenges we see with virtual shifts in learning environments.

## At a National Level: The Learning and Employment Record

The federal government has taken an interest in skills-based learning and calls it the Learning and Employment Record, or LER, in a twenty-five-page report released in 2020.[26] The LER is described by a federal group called the T3 Innovation Network as being similar to electronic health records that follow you to and from your various health care providers.[27] These electronic records can include extremely specific data such as employment history, earnings, education experience, credentialing, and more. What is also impressive is that National Student Clearinghouse has maintained a repository of nearly all college and many high school student transcripts for more than thirty years and is now interested in adding skills to those transcripts.[28] With all of this attention, one can imagine that incorporating skills into the transcript credentials that a student takes away from the college years is not that far off in the future. For example, IBM said in 2022 that it hired more than half of its workforce based on skills rather than on classical college transcripts.[29] Companies like Credential Engine have entered this space to provide services to, as they say on their website, "empower people to discover and pursue the learning and career pathways that are best for them."[30]

Lessons from these few examples and the LER are many. First, there is a market for companies to work with colleges and universities to meet a student's need for postgraduate employment without having to supply all of that experience themselves. While an in-house effort from a higher education institution could be better in theory, these external relations are the shape of the future if only because of their mastery of technology. Second, while we started this chapter with a discussion of technology putting information in the hands of students and their families, this technology also extends what a college education can be by helping the students get needed skills they can marry to their academic majors.

Whereas in the past that education was left up to the schools to provide with their history of defined programs, this technology helps the student play a much more active role in their own education by getting the feel for career paths in the real world. Done properly, it is a win for both the student and for the colleges and universities. Students get and grow from real-world experiences, and colleges can keep their focus on their basic class structure without having to bear the expense of becoming a cooperative education school. They can still have that impact that draws students to their campuses literally or virtually, which is especially important today when enrollment declines are causing some institutions to actually close. We predict that it will not be long before big technology companies develop an interest in this higher education market. But it will need constant attention from higher education folks, and we are sure there will be twists and turns in the road, perhaps some of them unfortunate.

## The Role of Governments in Actually Supporting Workplace Internships in College

The role of any national government is to defend its populace. That is why governments have police forces and armies, collect taxes, and build roads. More recently, some governments have taken an interest in helping their citizens get the most out of college in terms of having employment (and paying taxes) when they graduate. That helps the country in an increasingly information-rich world where the combination of knowledge and skills makes for a stronger economy. Who does not want that? We see this trend in the LER discussed earlier, and more is happening all over the world. This is a view coming from one of us as a longtime member of WACE.[31]

As an example outside the US, consider the country of Thailand, a longtime member of WACE and its national equivalent, the Thai Association of Cooperative Education, or TACE.[32] In Thailand, the government has taken a leadership position in coordinating and supporting the efforts of the universities and companies inviting WACE representatives to help them develop their program.[33] Here, the former education minister—who was the head of TACE for years—told us when he went there with a team to train the first generation of cooperative education coordinators in their universities, the goal was economic development so that Thailand would become the "Germany of Southeast Asia" through a properly educated workforce. The same practice of government leadership occurs in other countries like South Africa with organizations like SASCE[34] or in Australia with the Australian Collaborative Education Network (ACEN[35]), to name a few. Such practice occurs all over the world.

Speaking of Germany, a European economic powerhouse, there are programs where students join a university and a company at the same time. This arrangement is called Duale Hochschule Baden-Württemberg (DHBW) because of its location base,[36] and it works best for technical fields like engineering. DHBW students learn theory and facts from the classroom but application and practice from the workplace. It is a highly integrated form of cooperative education, but unlike in the practice in America and elsewhere, the choice of the worksite is not left to later determination.

Back in America, the Cooperative Education and Internship Association, or CEIA,[37] is a national organization committed to connecting colleges and universities that provide cooperative education and internships and allowing them to learn from each other. Their efforts support this national development the way Cooperative Education and Work-Integrated Learning (CEWIL) already does with federal funding in Canada, as discussed below.

The widespread global adoption of work periods that are integrated into the college years puts pressure on other colleges and universities in many countries to prepare their students in a similar fashion and let those work periods drive the student's growth as well as their maturity for later employment. It also puts pressure on universities in America and elsewhere to have their students study abroad or even do cooperative education abroad, but this is beyond the scope of this book (even though many employers are now global in their reach). What is not so remote is an aggressive experiential education program on America's northern border.

In Canada, the cooperative education support society CEWIL has worked with the federal government to develop an investment plan through the provinces.[38] For example, in Ontario, through Waterloo University—the largest cooperative education school in Canada—employers can get help accessing government funding to hire the interns that this university produces.[39] The companies get a 25 percent tax credit, up to $3000 CAD for a four-month internship term, and they can do it repeatedly so as to maintain a more continuous position. The overall investment started in 2017 with funds to help support and encourage sixty thousand students to get internships.[40] Clearly, Canada is supporting if not pushing experiential education for all or most of its college students. This is also seen in a 2013 185-page report[41] by the Higher Education Quality Council of Ontario, whose 5-page executive summary is worth reading.

In America, that Canadian practice of federal funding does not occur today. Although federal support for cooperative education did exist for a while (from 1965 to 1992) with the Higher Education Act,[42] it did not continue, and many institutions cut back or stopped the practice when the funding ended. For example, Queens College, CUNY, moved its cooperative education program into its career center when federal funding ended.[43]

It may seem ironic that the cooperative education idea, as mentioned, began in America over one hundred years ago, first at the University of Cincinnati and then quickly followed by Northeastern, Drexel, and other universities according to a history compiled by the CEIA.[44] The CEIA is the main American body now that WACE has moved to Canada and clarified that it is a global organization. Such organizations and many cooperative education programs in engineering and business schools (and in other disciplines) make the case for more blending of work experiences with the classic college education.

In high school, this idea of combining work and study has also been attempted. For example, a very successful program of that nature is Jobs for America's Graduates (JAG).[45] As of 2024 and for over forty years, JAG has helped 1.7 million high school students have work experiences while in high school. In just 2023 alone, in some thirty-six states and in more than 1,500 programs, they helped almost eighty thousand students (often from poor socioeconomic backgrounds) graduate with work experience in local companies. Rather than drop out, these JAG students graduate at about a 93 percent rate, which is above the national average for high school. What happens is that they get inspired by their work/earning potential, see the value in studying, and become more mature, just like what we see in college students. All of this maturity comes just from working in an industry with a sponsor for a few hours a week. But of course, high school students have brains too, and we do not think they are that different from those of college students.

## Summary

Technology is inescapable. But it provides ways to address needs that have long been in higher education's history. This can help deal with a trend toward integrating more direct experience with higher education, which is also inescapable. With technology, the good thing is that these needs for skills and professional growth can be incorporated today in an industry that has long been seen as the ivory tower, with outside being the real world. How we do use AI to support our goals was seen in another recent podcast where AI was again mentioned in not only helping gather data on an issue but providing a causal analysis of what to do about that problem.[46] Perhaps this approach helps the student applicant looking for a college that fits them, but it also helps colleges and universities determine which programs to develop to attract today's students. The more higher education can know about its market and what to do about it, the better it can serve them. Another question that AI might not be able to answer is how a faculty steeped in a successful past tradition adapts what it does best—developing the life of the mind—to developing the skills that students also want.

Chapter 10

# Back to the Brain: Neocortical Re-Representation, Explicit Thinking, and Neocortical Symbolic Logic

If you made it this far in the book, congratulations. Now you have a basic idea about how experiential activities can complement the good facts-and-theories education as delivered through a classically structured college education. We could leave it here. But we think it is important, with this knowledge that you now have, to revisit something that makes experiential education natural: the way the brain works. In this chapter, we are going to go a little deeper into basic ways we all make decisions, not the least of which is the college or university to attend or the course of study to pursue that will become a sustaining and fulfilling career after graduation. If we've sparked a bit of neuroscience curiosity in your mind, then this chapter is for you. If not, just skip to the conclusions at the end of this chapter.

## Two Brains in the Head

At least two brains are in the head, as we introduced in chapter 2 and built upon in the following three chapters. To briefly review, one part of the brain is the cognitive thinking brain that works explicitly or abstractly and uses symbolic logic, like reading and speaking. It is the part of the brain that makes concrete plans about which you can talk. It primarily resides in the part of the brain that we developed most recently in our evolution, the neocortex, and it is unique to humans. Touch your forehead. Just below your fingertips on the other side of the skin and skull is the frontal cortex. This region is built in utero through a highly complex migration of newly formed neurons guided by support cells called glial cells into a perfectly organized, six-layered pattern whose complexity is unparalleled in our technology (even by AI). Again, this brain region develops the plans and abstract contemplations that allow you to do higher-order thinking and speaking and make you who you are today.

The other part of the brain is the limbic system in the midbrain. It is the part of the brain that reacts emotionally and, you guessed it, it's right in the middle of your brain. It is implicit, reactive, and often obscured a bit from your cognition. This part of the brain helps make sure you keep your body fed and your thirst satiated to keep you at a normal functioning level. We call that homeostasis. It keeps the body's cells supported by blood that is of a proper composition. If that blood gets too salty, for example, you develop a powerful thirst motivation, find some water, and correct that imbalance.

In addition to these motivations and signals for self-preservation, the limbic system also brings value judgments into those cognitive plans. It enters into the feelings that you have about your decisions, like what college to attend and what to study there. Is this major right for you, or did your last internship suggest you would be happier with a different major and career? As mentioned in chapter 2, Daniel Kahneman referred to these two processes as system 1 (what we would call emotional) and system 2 (what we would call symbolic). But he would never say that they were connected to the brain in the way we just described. He preferred to stay at the behavioral decision level and leave the brain analysis to neuroscientists, like us.

We, your coauthors, really do believe that it is the interaction between these two broad brain areas that supports the beginning of professional wisdom growth in college and in all fields, even if you do not go to college. Assuming you do go to college, we believe that experience is where you best get a feel for the field you want to join, whether you are a surgeon, carpenter, businessperson, or poet. As we said in chapter 6, it is that trait of professional wisdom that hiring managers or postsecondary graduate admissions committees look for when interviewing prospective employees or students after they meet basic technical criteria. It is what experiential educators want to develop when they recommend students engage not only in experiences like an internship but also in reflection on an internship experience in college.[1] We could have called it "maturity," but that is a bit too broad. For us, the words "professional wisdom" combine the integration of symbolic cognitive knowledge from the classroom with the felt, gut-level knowledge of applying that learning in the real world.

## The Neocortex Structure and Function: First, Its Columns

The neocortex is clearly the brain's signature evolutionary accomplishment, at least from our human perspective. This brain structure has grown more than any other in proportion to total brain size. It is obviously important and has led to our dominance in the history of our planet, for better or worse. What is it about the cortex that was not in the rest of the brain that made it so important? The answer is again the symbolic processing of information, and we suggest that it depends upon the cortex's unique structure in the evolutionary history of cortical columns.

The development of the cortex is interesting and complex. In utero, the cortex develops from a layer of stem cells (rapidly dividing cells that can differentiate into anything) and with each division (think of one cell splitting into two), at least one of these gets pushed out onto the surface of the developing structure. It is through this process that we can make our brains thicker. Only the cells on the innermost layer have the ability to divide, though, so the "daughters" as they are called migrate out and form layers. So, these layers are made of neurons and they are guided to their appropriate locations by supporting cells that we call glial cells. Glial cells make a sort of scaffolding to guide migrating neurons to their target locations. The target is ultimately within a cortical column, which is a grouping that has less than two hundred neurons in it, spanning through these six layers of cortex. Within the columns, there is intense communication between those neurons, with some layers primarily receiving input (layer 4) and some layers primarily generating output (layer 5) to other brain areas, often to other cortical columns.

The thickness of each of these layers and what they are doing in detail is beyond the scope of this book, but two facts are worth mentioning. The first is from long ago when early neuroscientists like Brodmann noticed variations in thickness of these layers and in the size and type of neurons that made up each layer.[2] What was surprising and important is that this layering structure seemed to relate to function. For example, consider the place in the back of the brain where, after visual information comes in from the eye and is relayed to the cortex by a deep brain structure called the thalamus, this information pathway projects to your primary visual cortical processing area. In this primary visual cortical region, layer 4 is thick, and it runs that way until there is an abrupt transition to another visual processing part of the brain, the secondary visual cortical region. That secondary visual region takes its input from the primary area and does not have such a thick layer.[3] It is obvious if you look at a histological section of the stained brain, as Brodmann did long ago. The secondary visual area is doing something different. It seems to be continuing to work on developing a representation of your visual experience. If I asked you to close your eyes and envision your grandmother's face, this area or still higher areas would be what is active, rather than the primary visual area. Before we go further, let's consider a simple example of this visual processing that goes toward cognition.

As mentioned earlier, a rolling ball is tracked by the eyes through non-cortical systems that we humans share with lizards (who do not have much cortex). It is called the superior colliculus, is back in the brain stem, and appears to be able to at least keep eyes on target.[4] When that ball rolls behind a screen, we human adults jump our eyes to the other side and wait for the ball to come out and at the right time. If that does not happen, we express surprise. Even six-month-old babies do that. But a younger baby (as well as a lizard) waits for the ball to appear before jumping their eyes to the other side of the screen. They leave their eyes where the ball disappeared until it reappears. The difference is that with our advanced neocortex, we have a concept of trajectory. The very young baby and the lizard do not have that trajectory concept. It is the property of the cortex. Here we can see interplay between the visual regions of the brain and others outside of the occipital lobe, giving us a higher evolutionary ability to have a representation of where an object is going.

Somehow, to make such a symbolic representation, the neural processing was handed off from cortical column to cortical column and from one cortical region to another. Our seemingly safe speculation is that the concept of a trajectory is very important. How else do you think you could conclude the direction of a bear walking in the woods at night from sound alone if you did not have a trajectory concept? It is probably important to object permanence, the belief an object still exists when it is out of sight, something that develops in babies at the same time of about six months of age. This gives the classic game of peekaboo with a baby a whole new level of complexity. But more important is to know where a big predator is going, even in the dark, where one has to use hearing to make that judgment. In that instance, we would use a similar association with hearing the sound of a stick breaking, recognizing that whatever it is sounds big, orienting in that direction, and a bunch of other complex behavior patterns throughout numerous brain regions just to again find and track that threat.

So, what is it about the neocortex's columns that gives this brain structure the special ability to make a trajectory concept out of eye tracking, sound tracking, or better yet, our human ability to have symbolic logic underlying our language? The truth is that we really do not know as neuroscientists, but there is a very interesting parallel to the way artificial neural networks have been simulated in current large language models that underlie AI. That is, this internal processing node of a computer-simulated neuron is itself interconnected within the layers between multiple layers that are arranged from input to output. Apparently, the more layers, the better. In a recent paper, ChatGPT was suggested to have ninety-six layers of networked, simulated artificial neurons.[5] While it is not our purpose here to explain how neural networks process information or how ChatGPT actually learns from input, it is interesting that we seem to learn from input. No one explicitly taught us language when we were children. Our parents and older speakers with whom we interacted did offer us corrections and examples, but few if any of them were trained as language experts. We learned from that input of the world and so did AI in programs such as ChatGPT; we both have this unique structure of repeated and interconnected processing. However, we have more neurons (approximately eighty-six billion), and they are real, not simulated in a computer. We also have many, many millions of cortical columns that some people think are grouped together in what are called "megacolumns" (still in the millions). We actually wrote a blog about this topic[6] and about how the frontal cortex tries to read the limbic system processes to create a value component to decision-making.[7] Maybe that is why, at least at this point, we are still the inventors of AI computer technology and not the other way around.

## The Neocortex Structure and Function: Its Interconnected Columns

Another feature of our neocortex, particularly in us humans and higher-level primates, is the massive interconnections between our cortical structures. The main neural component of communication is called the axon. It does long-distance communication between neurons, and it has a particular property of being myelinated (wrapped in the lipid or fat layers of other cells) that gives it a white appearance. Hence why its connections are called white matter. These white matter connections between our cortical columns and brain regions allow us to perform remarkable feats. They are the reason that the front of the brain can communicate to the back (and left to right), and they are also why superficial layers can communicate to much deeper, evolutionarily conserved regions.

An example is how when you put your hand in your pocket and feel one of your keys, you instantly have a visual image in your mind of what it would look like if you could see it with your eyes. This is called "cross-modal" sensory transfer because it goes between the two senses of touch and vision. It is a very interesting property that lower animals struggle to show, even monkeys to some extent. It allows you to predict what your pet cat will feel like, look like, sound like, and so on from your experience of any one of the senses or from just your imagination. Your cat, on the other hand, likely only processes you as that kind of a unified entity when you are physically present because the cat's network of cortical interconnection is less rich, and of course its neocortex is a bit smaller than yours, even proportional to its size. On the flip side, we bet that even when you aren't with your cat, you can visualize them, hear the sound of their meow, and even imagine the feeling of their fur—perhaps even eliciting a positive emotional response. Meanwhile, your cat is likely just waiting by the food bowl for their dinner.

These networks, processing centers, and interconnections in the brain give us our high-level abilities. For example, remember the default mode network from chapter 3? It turns on when we do not have a task and our mind is wandering a bit. Here is where the default mode network becomes active. It seems to connect the planning properties of our frontal lobe with the object recognition properties of our parietal and other object-representing lobes in the back of the brain. It is widespread in connections. Why might we have that network? Well, suppose you as the reader are waiting for someone outside their office and you do not take out your phone. You might use that time to do a little planning. Perhaps you need to stop at the grocery store on the way home, where you will have just enough time to pick up that gallon of milk because you ran out that morning. You can see yourself going through the store to the milk area, picking up the gallon of milk (it might even feel cold in your mind), and heading to the checkout. But think about what these connections do when the default mode network is not turned on. Were those "wires" just sitting there waiting for the chance to let your mind wander through such a little plan?

## Connections Between the Cortex and Deeper Brain Structures: Cortical-Limbic Integration

If the neocortex represents the outside world and has developed advanced networks to communicate between its columnar processing centers, why wouldn't it also receive input from and talk to other noncortical brain areas? Consider, for example, that you are waiting patiently in the waiting room for a job interview. As the clock ticks closer to the time of the appointment, you finally hear your name and are escorted by the human resources officer waiting for you into your potentially new boss's office. How did you know to place your feet like that so you moved gracefully and did not fall down? Who organized that, and who is in charge of the feet? Your mind was on your racing heart, posture, and the elevator pitch that you had been running through on repeat in your head for the past several days. You did not think about your feet. Some lower brain structure did that. You trained that brain structure long ago when you were a toddler and refined it when you were an adolescent in the soccer league. Now it works effortlessly even though the computations are complex. But you do remain in charge (or your cortex does), and you could have hop-skipped over to meet your new boss (although they might have thought you were weird if you did that and maybe you wouldn't have gotten the job). The legs are yours and you can do anything you want with them, but they retain some control to help you manage balance and maybe take a small step up as you walk into the office. The same is true for your limbic system, except now you are keeping track of your feelings. Is this job interview your dream job or something that you are only interviewing for because a friend recommended it?

Simply put, the neocortex seems to re-represent the processing of the older evolutionary limbic (emotional) structures. They are there and integrated with your cognitive thinking, just like your voluntary movements are integrated with the lower motor system in the example we just mentioned. So, if your amygdala is detecting a fear situation or your accumbens is detecting a reward situation, your cortex integrates it and can make predictions with it. It makes sense—the advanced cortical processing areas can do more complex functions. Also, if we look closely at the arrangement of these deeper, more evolutionarily conserved brain structures, we do not see the highly sophisticated layering and columns that we see in the neocortex. While these structures are made of neurons and have important connectivity to other regions, they do not parallel the processing ability that the human cortex holds.

Deeper brain structures, because of their importance and evolutionarily conserved nature, have been the subject of a massive body of research. A typical reductionist approach to science is to take a complex phenomenon and break it down into its simplest components. That is what both of your coauthors did specifically with the reward circuit during their PhDs studying a midbrain reward-related neurotransmitter called dopamine. Reward is a complicated thing, especially if you think about liking or disliking something—that is driven by reward. But if you think about the craving and cue-induced behavior that we see in individuals that suffer from a substance abuse disorder, that expands far beyond "I like this" or "I do not like this." This is where we see that neural communication with our cortical structures. We mentioned previously that this communication between our basic "like" and "dislike" limbic circuits, which might come from an excellent internship at a law firm or a not-so-fun shadowing experience in a hospital, does transmit the conclusion to the neocortex but does not show how they reached that judgment, the why. That is the job of the thinking, planning neocortex to figure out from that like/dislike input. At this point, we have to stop because this is not a book about neuroscience, but there is plenty to read here and for additional insight, we like to write blogs about such cortical-limbic integration (see our blog called "The Other Lobe of the Brain").[8] But the point is, how does this reactive midbrain experience of the accumbens or the amygdala get connected with the symbolic reasoning of the neocortex? That is another interesting story.

With the advent of modern brain scanners, we are learning more every day about these connections and how processing of the limbic system impacts the cortex, so we can explicitly think about it and certainly talk about it. This is the kind of brain scan work that we think will eventually bring the understanding developed by Daniel Kahneman and his colleagues (remember system 1 and system 2 underlying decisions?) together with an understanding of some of the brain's function. For now, we are left with some tantalizing ideas and are learning more and more about brain areas.

## Connections Within the Cortex Are Just as Important: Cognitive-Emotional Integration

Let's start with the ventromedial prefrontal cortex. There are many neocortical regions that directly connect with deeper brain circuits, but why do we pick that one? To start, it was made famous by the behavioral neurologist. As mentioned previously, Damasio argued that the famous philosopher René Descartes was incomplete when he said, "I think, therefore I am." According to Damasio, what Descartes should have said is, "I feel, therefore I can think, therefore I am." Our feelings give us the judgment that we have reached a logical conclusion. It is where the classic "aha" moment comes from that we have all felt before.

What may have given Damasio the basic idea is a patient he saw who had damage to his ventromedial prefrontal cortex. This patient was intellectually normal and could discuss with high quality, for example, the rivalry between two sports teams. But if one asked the patient to make what seemed to be a simple decision where a judgment was required, a feeling needed to make a decision, he was paralyzed. Damasio's example was in asking the patient, "When would be better for the next appointment—a day next week or a day the week after?" The patient appeared to have tried to figure it out logically, even down to the fact that the weather reports were more accurate for next week than the week after. But neither you nor we would have done that. We would have said something like "next week should work," buying a little time for planning, and the task would have been done. The idea here is that in making this decision symbolically or logically, the neocortex would have been influenced by the input of the emotional system even though it does not have columns. However, it is when the neocortex conjured up a scenario that the limbic system could react as though it were real and give the feeling.

To make this more clear, let's discuss a particular area: the insula cortex, a brain area with rich connections to not only the body's internal state but also to the ever-so-emotional fear headquarters, the amygdala. You may have heard the expression "once burned, twice shy." That can be thought of as the amygdala doing simple conditioning between two events: You touched the hot stove and you got burned. So, do not do that again. But what if you have to cook dinner? You must be near the stove with hot burners and hot pans. So, what do you do? Your neocortex prepares you by wearing a cooking glove and/or turning the handles of the pots so they will not be over the burners where they could pick up heat. You minimize the risk. Your insular cortex is connected to the amygdala and so are other cortical areas. You can work around the potential risks and not get burned when you make dinner. In a similar way, the insula (and other brain areas) manage risk every day so you can live a life free of fear but still go into situations where you could be hurt . . . unless maybe you had a terrible experience and now have post-traumatic stress disorder from that particular circumstance. Then you might need more than just the insula cortex to help get you back to a better life.

We see this integration grow as we age as well, which directly correlates to the volume of our prefrontal cortex and our amygdala. This explains the impulsivity that we see in, for example, a twelve-year-old boy as he acts out and gets on a streak of skipping school. Despite his parents' attempts to convince him of the importance of school, it seems almost as if there's no way to get him to stop. That is because the prefrontal cortex is home to the explicit stream of thought that, like an angel on your shoulder, is saying something along the lines of "If you don't stop this behavior, then you are messing up your opportunity to get into a good college and earn a high-paying career." All of that involves extremely sophisticated understanding and even more projected planning, so it's easy to see why a twelve-year-old may not comprehend the implications of his actions. Take that and pit it against a region that is, in relation to its mature adult size, much larger in proportion to the prefrontal cortex (the amygdala[9]), and it only makes sense as to why his impulsive behavior is winning out.

The white matter tract that connects amygdala to the prefrontal cortex, more specifically the orbitofrontal region, is called the uncinate fasciculus. Without this pathway, not only would the twelve-year-old boy struggle with regulating emotional responses; he would also not be able to form appropriate social relationships and maintain a state of emotional well-being. The interesting thing about this pathway is that functional imaging studies, specifically of adolescents, has shown that the thicker this white matter tract (which we discussed earlier is a feature of linked cortical columns), the better integration and regulation of emotional responses.[10]

So, in addition to the size of the brain regions of the prefrontal cortex and the amygdala, we see a similar pattern with the changes in structural development of the communication link between these two regions influencing that higher-order, emotional "Do this because it's fun at the moment" and cognitive "This is a bad choice for me and my future" processing. We hope by the time that our college-aged students are tasked with making decisions about their future, all of these brain regions are at or close to their full adult size, allowing them to appropriately integrate all of this higher-order information.

Neuroscientists have studied this and have tried to parse out the separate processes of cognition and emotion, including many pieces of the prefrontal cortex and amygdala relationship we see here, but find it challenging because of the entangled representations that are coded by multiple cognitive and emotional variables.[11] This is again where our networks come in, but adding on the fact that these regions develop at different speeds throughout adolescence and are shaped by experience, you can see what a challenge our scientists are up against in studying this cognitive-emotional integration thing. Also, this is only a small piece of the huge body of examples of this communication, albeit the ones we have mentioned have received a bit more attention than other areas of this cortical-limbic neurocircuitry.

## Back to Professional Wisdom

A quote we used earlier comes back to us now: A cynic is someone "who knows the price of everything and the value of nothing." Our cortical-limbic and cognitive-emotional integration is designed to make us not cynics. It is designed, we argue, to give us sophisticated insight about risks and values that we might call a part of wisdom. This is why this book has the words "Professional Wisdom" in the title. A college student goes on an internship and not only gets a feel for what that field might offer if they were to continue with that major and enter that career path, but by integrating their classical classroom academic knowledge with that experience they get value judgments on those cognitive plans and start to show that wisdom. One of our goals now is to try to study those cortical brain areas that underlie integration with the limbic system. The idea here is to see how the neocortex elevates the older emotional reactive experiences to a more symbolic level. So, fear becomes managed risk, positive experiences become controlled activities (not compulsive behaviors), and all of these feelings get incorporated into sophisticated cognitive plans.

According to legend, the king of Syracuse asked the polymath Archimedes to estimate whether his crown was made of just gold or contained some measure of the lighter silver. This would have been a simple matter of weighing the crown and seeing if the volume compared with the weight was enough. But Archimedes could not melt down the crown to get that volume measurement. This was important as Archimedes, the great scientist, could not disappoint the king. So, when he was getting into a bathtub, he noticed that his body caused the water to go up in the tub. That difference in the water level was a measure of his volume. At that moment, he purportedly yelled "Eureka!" (I have discovered it),[12] jumped out of the tub, and ran naked through the streets. He had discovered that all he had to do was put the crown in a container of water, which he safely could do, and compare its measured weight to the volume of water it displaced, and he had his answer. The story, even if not true, has entered into the scientific legend so that the word "eureka" has been incorporated into the general literature with stories about other discoveries. We tell it to you here because of the undeniable emotional reaction to the cognitive/symbolic operation of making a discovery.

## How This Plays into the Feel of a Career

The old book *Zen and the Art of Motorcycle Maintenance* is more about getting the feel for life than it is about motorcycles. As we mentioned, but it bears repeating, there is one telling passage where the narrator is attaching the cowl on his motorcycle with a screw and talks about how he has a mechanic's feel for how hard to turn the screw so it will stay put without stripping the threads. This comes through as a metaphor for the feel of many decisions in life. As mentioned in previous chapters, *Practical Wisdom* by Barry Schwartz[13] talks about learning from experience, including failure, about what is the right thing or wise thing to do in a situation as opposed to how to just follow the rules. This is especially useful if something happens that is unexpected—something that is not in the plan.

At a conference of cooperative education practitioners long ago, a surgeon who was also a university president talked about the value of experience and compared it to his own apprenticeship (really a medical internship) he did with experienced surgeons. At first, he remarked that he had difficulty telling the internal organs apart. Jim was there and remembers him saying "everything looked pink." Eventually he linked the book knowledge from earlier in his training with what he was learning on the internship. He learned how to wield a scalpel in the body. He then had felt knowledge, was professionally wise in this context, and if he were our surgeon, we would be glad for it. Again, this is what the hiring manager, we believe, detects in a college student job applicant who has had a few internships versus one who is just book smart and applying for the first time.

We all do this in large or small parts. Our feelings ride along with our cognitive operations, and the neocortex incorporates them in ways that we probably underestimate, focusing more on the symbolic logic itself and less on the lower limbic guidance to that cognition. Yet it is this integration that seems to bequeath to a person that professional wisdom that we think is best begun in college, before the student commits themselves to a career or to time and money in further education that leads to that career. There is much research to be done in this space, and we are by no means experts here, nor will we be placing our college students in brain scanners before and after an internship experience to identify where this professional wisdom comes from. But we do know that the brain can accomplish extraordinary things, and the proper integration of information driven by experience is necessary for student success.

## Summary

We believe that a good way to gain this direct experience is to simply do something in the real-world that indexes that subsequent career plan, such as an internship. We also think that cognitive reflection on the experience is very helpful in allowing the cortex to better engage with and perhaps re-represent the emotional reactions that come with experiences. While the exact mechanisms by which the brain executes these cortical-limbic and cognitive-emotional integrations is unknown, we know they occur, and we must encourage those processes through learning from experience. Ultimately, it is the obligation of higher education itself to create opportunities, varied and many, for their students to engage in these activities so that they can begin to develop this professional wisdom to choose wisely (even without a eureka moment) and to develop that beginning projection of wisdom to gain the admission or employment that should follow the college experience. That is a win-win for the student and the college or university that makes them both stronger. And that is our eureka moment.

Chapter 11

# What Colleges and Universities Can Do to Develop Professional Wisdom

By now you can see that professional wisdom is a natural property of the brain. It occurs in developing college students and serves them well in college classes, as they seem to have a more mature attitude toward learning. It works particularly well as they go into the next phase of their careers, either into a profession or on to further schooling. Here they will be judged again, like they were when getting into a college, but this time it is much more serious, as the competition is tougher and the commitment is longer. Here is where they really need professional wisdom as an attribute.

Years ago, outside of cooperative education schools or vocationally oriented colleges and programs, getting these supplemental experiential activities was largely left to the students themselves. A college education was about the life of the mind, and by that we mean it was about the life of the cognitive brain. The emotional mind was left to figure out for itself what a good career path would be. As we have seen in this book, though, experiences affect both parts of the brain, and cognitive-emotional integration between them is needed to not only figure out where in the career world one fits as a student but also to develop the beginning of that professional wisdom for oneself. Industry has long called for it. Now, the public is demanding it (or its result of employability). Colleges and universities have to justify themselves in terms of the investment of time and money by the family in an ever more demanding environment. As a recent paper by the Upjohn Institute for Employment Research on the higher education industry's response to the labor market states, "nearly three-quarters of jobs over the next decade will require postsecondary education."[1]

What is really going to put pressure on higher education in the future is AI. As we discussed in chapter 9, we believe that AI will use big data analytics from national labor databases and others to provide the individual student applicant with a personalized higher education institutional ranking. Some of this analysis is happening now (mentioned in that same Upjohn Institute paper[2]), and it is not hard to imagine that such data could be turned into an institutional ranking. Any such ranking data is yet to be personalized to the individual applicant even though it does have the potential to generate a ranking of schools on the basis of their reactions to the labor market.

What we see as a personalized AI ranking again could include many of the college education characteristic variables that we now have about admissions: faculty research, admissions profile, graduation rates, job placement rates, experiential learning opportunities, tuition price, institutional resources, and so on. It will also include the data we just mentioned, such as that on economic social mobility outcomes and job placements. But the big difference in the new personalized AI rankings, we suggest, will include the applicant's individual profile and career interests. Using that information, we think this new profile-based ranking can focus even more on postcollege career outcomes for students, which will make these outcome statistics even more powerful.

Such statistics on success could involve reports on getting such students into the jobs or graduate programs they identified as desirable. Of course, we believe that getting good rankings of success in this personalized AI system will involve experiential education opportunities that complement the classical academic features of a good academic college education. Otherwise, the ranking will show that the institution is not helpful, and what institution wants that negative tag on their personalized AI ranking presentation? Ironically, we believe that these complementary experiential activities combined with classical academic learning will eventually be seen as teaching something that AI cannot do, what one cooperative education university president called "robot-proof" education[3] or, in our words, the beginning of professional wisdom.

So, given the market pressures from enrollment needs and budget challenges, the question remains as to what colleges and universities specifically need to do to build up their students' professional wisdom development through direct experiential activities and other operations.

## Better Use of College Career Services Offices

To start, let's reexamine the development of the career office and the higher education societies that support those offices. Today, general organizations such as NACE have embraced career readiness programs,[4] and an example is their resource "Competencies for a Career-Ready Workforce."[5] That document, among others, lays out what students get out of these experiences; for example, under the Career and Self-Development section, they mention that students learn to "show an awareness of [their] own strengths and areas for development" and "professionally advocate for oneself and others." There are seven other sections in that document—Communication, Critical Thinking, Equity and Inclusion, Leadership, Professionalism, Teamwork, and Technology—and each section contains a set of sample behaviors. Documents like this exist in various places and in more academic research centers like the Institute for Experiential Learning that is based on the research of David Kolb,[6] a well-known experiential education thinker.

The history of career services offices goes back to early vocational learning institutions, but they probably got their start with the GI Bill, which sent many armed services members to college following World War II in the 1940s. Later, in the 1970s, career counseling began to develop and blossomed into the "dynamic networking hubs" we see today that use a lot of technology to help students find their way.[7] In all of the institutions with which we have been affiliated that are not cooperative education institutions, these career offices try to entice students to come in early in their college years and not wait until the end to begin thinking about a resume or LinkedIn profile or even an internship.

In our experience, the message tends not to work as well as it could, perhaps because it is not institution-wide. Most institutions follow the old pattern of classroom-based, academic program–driven education where advisors and faculty focus on the content in those programs. Other activities are typically considered extracurricular. Career services centers come to mind as the student nears the end of their time in college. That denies students the chance to learn about themselves and their career paths from direct experience. While career services is trying to increase their presence and integrate earlier into students' academic careers, a survey from Inside Higher Ed in 2024 points out that at least a third of college graduates report never once utilizing any career services opportunities.[8] Of those that did utilize career services, they were 2.8 times more likely to report that their degree was worth the price they paid for it.[9] Clearly, there is more work here to be done in really tapping into the value of these offices, especially when it improves the alumni value of the education.

Another recent report from Inside Higher Ed recommends that career services offices become fully student-centric.[10] After all, the students are the customers. Some ways in which we see this as a possibility would be to meet students where they are and bring the resources to them. This could include enhancing employer partnerships by building long-term relationships with local, national, and international employers. Regularly inviting them to campus for recruitment events, workshops, and panels can help with this. Advisory boards with employers to get feedback on how to better prepare students for the workforce could also be a tool for this. Customized recruitment, such as offering targeted resume books and exclusive interview slots to employers, could also facilitate these relationships.

Career services offices can also increase student engagement by focusing on early and frequent interactions. Colleges and universities should start engaging with students early in their college careers, ideally from their first year. They should offer workshops on career exploration, resume writing, and networking. Career ambassadors or peer advisors could also be utilized. This would include training a group of students to serve as peer advisors, helping their classmates navigate career services and offering peer-led workshops. As many college students would agree, including an incentive for participation, such as certifications, badges, or credits for attending career workshops or participating in career-related programs, will increase attendance at events as well.

For those who are not comfortable attending career services events, there is a possibility to integrate career services directly into the curriculum of career-related courses. Topics could include career readiness, such as personal branding, networking, and industry-specific job search strategies. In this approach, faculty could integrate career-related learning into their coursework and even potentially cosponsor events that link academic learning with career skills. Faculty may see this as a win-win, as we receive many career-related questions during our one-on-one advising sessions or in office hours each semester. As to make the best of everyone's time, this approach can lessen the commitment of everyone involved while still giving the students good guidance.

Tailoring support resources to specific students takes a lot of time but will help with outcomes. While we mentioned that these offices may not have enough staff or support, offering one-on-one counseling sessions tailored to students' career goals, academic backgrounds, and personal interest is becoming more critical than ever.[11] AI can help in personalizing the experience for the student. Ensuring that resources are available for a wide range of careers (including nontraditional paths, entrepreneurship, and international opportunities) is also necessary. More evidence is now emerging that career services offices must dedicate resources and events for diverse student populations, such as international students, first-generation students, and those with disabilities. These students fill a specific need in the professional world, with companies such as IBM, Merck & Co., Target, and Walmart creating pipelines to recruit and train diverse workers. Career services offices must follow suit and recognize the need in this space.[12]

We also believe that the modern application of an education partnered with a career-focused approach can happen and should involve technology. Reasons for that include the fact that most college students have a vigorous online presence. That presence, while developing in faculty, has not yet caught up with the students. Thus, the institution is just missing an opportunity. Second, this trend to provide work placement and other experiential opportunities has not been missed by startup technology companies. They have developed programs, apps, and other technology-based operations that can help students find internships. We have seen this in commercial applications of technology in hiring and in the developing federal LER.

Career services staff are not uneducated. On the contrary, in our experience, these offices are home to extremely qualified and hardworking individuals. Given the lack of institutional investment in their personnel, though, these centers have invested in companies that help to bridge this gap—and the students are beginning to jump on board and tap into the resources these companies have to offer. The only question is when the rest of the college or university operations will catch up and see these internship activities as helping develop their students and not as something that is extracurricular, that at best just takes time away from studying and at worst is a distraction from learning. We will know when this moment has arrived in any institution when the academic faculty, in general, has a pretty good familiarity with what the career services office does and works that knowledge into their mentoring (and, even better, into their classroom teaching).

## Better Use of College Alumni

The alumni at many universities have deep affection for the school and the current students that have followed them there. They like talking about their careers and even meeting students interested in what they do. The alumni relations office is very interested in building its own ties to the alumni, if only to encourage them to later make charitable donations to the institution after they get some discretionary resources. Indeed, in most universities, the alumni relations office is much bigger than the career services office. So, it is natural that these purposes can be comfortably combined. There just has to be a process to coordinate the connection. While the career services office can handle bringing in companies that want to hire graduates and in doing so show them off to students interested in internships, the alumni need special handling.

An example of alumni involvement comes from the University at Albany, where your coauthors both met. It is called UCAN, which stands for UAlbany Career Advisory Network.[13] Alumni can sign up online to be mentors for undergraduates, and undergraduates can likewise easily register for UCAN and start browsing its alumni network. Once a connection is made, the student's career experience is potentially strengthened, and the alumni's connection with the university is potentially enhanced through doing some good work for its students. Over half of college graduates report that they did not have a mentor while in college because they didn't know how to find one,[14] and students are beginning to state that it is the responsibility of the college or university to find them one.[15] Well-organized alumni relations offices in cahoots with career services is one way to facilitate this. Many universities are now pushing this cooperation hard.

For example, UCAN does much more, from job boards and panel discussions to networking events, and is indeed highly connected to the career services office. Industry-specific career panels there and at many other universities and colleges allow students to hear advice from people immersed in the field and create relationships with them. Alumni-led skills workshops can allow students the opportunity to learn directly from professionals in the field, whether this be industry-specific or on broad topics such as resume building, interview techniques, and public speaking. Q&A or "Ask Me Anything" events allow students to ask alumni questions about their careers, industries, and professional experiences. After all, if our alumni are rich in professional wisdom, why not tap into that? All over America, such alumni organizations are being set up. Pretty soon, it will be a recruitment liability for your institution if it does not have such an office. And a serious one at that.

## Better Use of Emerging Technology

Technology can provide a partial answer to the natural expenses that cooperative education schools like Cincinnati, Northeastern, Drexel, and others have already (and long ago) built into their operating budgets. To a non–cooperative education university, with the current existing budget constraints, it is just too expensive to hire the personnel, at least without a massive external gift or a return to government funding. The college or university needs these people to nurture both the employer and the student in their relationships. Career services, at their typical funding level, are at least five and maybe ten times too small to carry that responsibility for all or most undergraduates. On the positive side, students and many young people have leveraged technology to shop, buy food, and so on. So, this is their world, and if properly applied, technology could meet their needs. The employers are already using hiring platforms like Indeed or ZipRecruiter to find employees. Maybe they can also get on board with applications like Handshake to hire interns. Maybe those interns will later become employees.

What is really needed is something like the LER (as discussed in chapter 9) that combines courses and skills (e.g., from internships) to present a new kind of resume. Again, companies are working on that, and we mentioned iQ4 in the area of cybersecurity and beyond. These job skills for almost all fields are documented on O*NET,[16] a website that is sponsored by the US Department of Labor. The question is not whether they exist or whether an AI-based program can sort them out for a student. The question for higher education is whether they can get these skills combined with academic knowledge into their students. Again, the ones that will stand tall in the competition by our speculated personal AI career ranking of colleges and universities will be the ones that can directly link to whatever is next for their undergraduates after graduation.

It is interesting that most already do this for their graduate students. Think how much time medical schools and related disciplines spend on giving their graduate students academic and clinical (e.g., practical) knowledge about patient care. How much effort do business schools put into ensuring their graduates do well in the workforce? Frankly, the same is true everywhere, even in many purely academic departments that want to show that a PhD is a ticket to employment, if not as a professor then in a related profession.

Technology must also be used for the assessment of existing career readiness programs. Sometimes, colleges and universities actually hire outside consultants to do this, or it is part of a state accreditation program.[17] Regardless of the means, the process is necessary. We mentioned some of them already. For example, Handshake helps career services officers guide students to find internships. InStage helps students hone their internship interview skills. iQ4 helps students develop their skills in the cybersecurity area by linking resumes to national job databases and even to university courses. There are many such companies that use technology to gather important information, organize it, and display it to students. As the pressure builds to have better postgraduation outcomes and as internships and other such activities rise in the life of college students, these companies can help universities and colleges better serve students in this new marketplace.

## Prioritize Faculty Mentoring in Addition to Teaching

The most significant personnel element of any college or university is its faculty. When real changes happen on campus, it is because the faculty embrace them and even lead them. Faculty impact all of the students and carry with them the imprint of the university. Many years ago, it was predicted that when online classes became popular in the 1990s,[18] the brick-and-mortar colleges and universities would disappear. This did not happen. There is something about the presence of faculty and students together (and of students together) that is important to learning and growing. We believe it is the personal contact that happens in the classroom. Humans are, after all, social beings. The interaction can spill over to mentoring relationships and can be very powerful when the mentor takes an interest in the student's ultimate growth. For example, most students we have mentored have asked us for recommendations for graduate school or employment, and mentors write good letters.

In research universities, often this mentoring takes the form of an undergraduate being invited into a professor's research world. There they interact with graduate students and other senior personnel but also with other undergraduates. True, the professor is making an investment of time (either on their own or with their people), but what higher education has learned over time, perhaps since the example of the MIT Undergraduate Research Opportunities Program (UROP),[19] is that there can be a payback in terms of research productivity. In these environments, an undergraduate grows, just like they do at an industry-based internship. But here they have one of their professors who might have taught (or will teach) one of their classes to see how they work. If the student has a professional interest (e.g., medicine, engineering, business), it can be much like working (e.g., hospital, engineering firm, company). Sometimes students do both. But the presence of a professor ties the student's experiential learning back to the institution and can inspire other students even if they cannot get that experience. Of course, there are more undergraduates than professors, but even if 10 percent of the student body did undergraduate research of some kind with all types of faculty, it could help the entire undergraduate program be more effective.

As we discussed, the ivory tower of higher education does not always prioritize saving space for these opportunities, especially among newer faculty. There is no line on the promotions packet as to how many letters of recommendation one has written in a year or how many hours outside of office hours the faculty member has spent guiding students with career choices. While the number of students in the lab is looked at, this focuses mainly on the number of graduate students (at least in research-active universities). We, at least, as your coauthors, serve as mentors and do not reserve mentorship for graduate students or students who do projects with us. Yet any professor will tell you that with twenty-four hours in a day and much to do and a ratio of many more students than professors, mentoring in the aggregate is hard.

Some colleges and universities are better at protecting time for faculty members to serve students outside of the classroom, whereas other institutions assign dozens and dozens of advisees to each faculty member, making it so that they can only have five to ten minutes with the student each semester to approve their proposed course schedule and nothing else. Some universities shield faculty from all advising and send them to professional advisors who do a good job—the best they can with an advising load that is often too high. There is a lot to be done here, and much that can be said, but we are getting beyond the scope of this book. However, we want to flag the power of faculty to help students, not just with instruction but with a little human contact through mentoring.

We do not want our institutions to be known as the ivory tower. We want institutions to be known for the excellent intellectual power and dedicated faculty that they are employing. After all, the institution hired these faculty for their scholarship, and they have to pursue it. But institutions are like people. They can "walk and chew gum at the same time." And most professors really do care about the students. So, it is a matter of encouragement up and down the academic hierarchy, from adjuncts to full professors. What happens when the institution does that is the students respond. Now, this will take a bit more time away from teaching and research, but clever places can find ways to incorporate undergraduates into the research, service, and leadership mission with faculty and also into the mission of the college or university itself.

Then, when the students respond as though the institution cares, they will also more likely engage with faculty, advisors, and their peers about why they came and what they want to do with their lives. That allows value propositions about intellectual topics and student career paths to be more easily exchanged. Conversations between the faculty and staff can turn into reflection on experiential or even course opportunities, and that can turn into mentoring. Now the ivory tower fades a bit, students are happier and even more productive in their classes as they begin to see what college could do for them, and maybe they even believe a bit more in themselves. That outcome drives retention, which makes senior administrators happy, as retention contributes to the budget as well as institutional reputation.

# Three Final Remarks from the Authors

## First, the Book Is Done and We Hope You Liked It

For us, it was a labor of love (our limbic systems). We tried to make the point that academic learning and experiential learning go hand in hand to make a more mature, prepared, and professional college graduate—hand in hand except for that fact that, as often stated here, "the heart has its reasons, which reason knows nothing of" (from Blaise Pascal). That means the head (the cognitive mind/brain) is going to have to reach out to the limbic or emotional brain, which is why most experiential educators incorporate reflection into experiential learning. This brings the explicit and implicit learning into a bit better alignment, although the heart's reasons are tricky and may only reveal themselves later or under strange circumstances. Still, it is better if the heart and the head work together, so you students have to talk about what you are thinking/feeling, and you faculty have to create opportunities—even though you are busy—to encourage that reflection and listen to it. Sometimes a word or two from someone older and wiser can make a big difference in your life. It did in ours, and maybe (hopefully) it did in yours. That is the ultimate cognitive-emotional integration and perhaps even something wise.

## Second, Professional Wisdom Is an Ally, Not an Enemy, of Pure Academic Learning

We hear this all the time, and it has come up in this book previously. So, we want to make clear here that the learning of our students, in most cases, is helped, not hurt, by a touch of the profession in the teaching and, importantly, in their experience. It is true that with their phones, students can fact-check us in real time as we faculty lecture, but there is something else that happens when they apply those principles themselves in a workplace. We get a tiny bit of that in the biology lab associated with the biology lecture, but imagine how much more they learn when that student does an internship at a biotech firm. The same goes for the law firm or business or community service project. We know seniors are typically more mature than freshmen. They did not get that way because they grew another lobe of their brain in college. They got that way through learning in and out of the classroom and pushing their boundaries with challenges beyond the current curricular requirements. All of these things foster an even stronger development of professional wisdom.

## Third, Professional Wisdom Confers Something That AI Does Not

As the science fiction writer Joanna Maciejewska once said, "I want AI to do my laundry and dishes so that I can do art and writing, not for AI to do my art and writing so that I can do my laundry and dishes."[1] The same is true for the jobs of the future. Our college graduates need human skills, and at this point, we believe that comes from applying skills to intellectual content and being able to see the value from emotional insights into processes and conclusions. That does not mean that AI does not hold great potential for our learners in developing all types of knowledge and wisdom. For us, though, in this professional wisdom world, we must be doing something to engage those brain circuits that extend much deeper than an AI-generated response will instill in our learners.

# Conclusion

As previously mentioned in a reference to the book *Practical Wisdom*,[1] that kind of thinking comes from experiences, from trying and even failing and then learning in a real-world application. With the highly refined classroom and academic structures of colleges and universities, they are not generally able to provide these real-world experiences. So, smart institutions are sending their students out into their future workplaces to get some initial implicit or gut-level learning to pair with their facts-and-theories learning from the classroom. As we like to say and have already said, you can give someone your grandmother's recipe for blueberry pie, and if the content transmission is perfect, that person can make a credible pie the first time. But everyone knows that after twenty pies, the product will be much better from learning by doing. This learning by doing idea has been said for years by leading educational thinkers such as John Dewey.[2] It is time to take this movement—still newish to some institutions yet old hand to others—and make it a central focus so that our students can have more professional wisdom. It will improve their own career outcomes and also those of the country. Borrowing from Peter Allen,[3] what is old (apprenticeship) is new again.

# Endnotes

## PREFACE

1. The Editors of Encyclopaedia Britannica. "Apprenticeship." Accessed May 8, 2025. https://www.britannica.com/topic/apprenticeship.
2. The Editors of Encyclopaedia Britannica. "University." Accessed May 8, 2025. https://www.britannica.com/topic/university.
3. Craig, Ryan. *Apprentice Nation: How the "Earn and Learn" Alternative to Higher Education Will Create a Stronger and Fairer America*. BenBella Books, 2023.
4. Wildavsky, Ben. *The Career Arts: Making the Most of College, Credentials, and Connections*. Princeton University Press, 2023.
5. Pirsig, Robert M. *Zen and the Art of Motorcycle Maintenance: An Inquiry*. Mariner Books, 2006.
6. Wikipedia contributors. "Lady Windemere's Fan." Wikipedia, The Free Encyclopedia. Last modified March 30, 2025. https://en.wikipedia.org/wiki/Lady_Windermere%27s_Fan.

## CHAPTER 1

1. Spencer, Rachel. "Why College Enrollment Is a Marketing Problem." AccessU. Accessed May 8, 2025. https://accessu.com/why-college-enrollment-is-a-marketing-problem/.
2. Siena College. "Home Page." Accessed May 8, 2025. https://www.siena.edu.
3. The College of Saint Rose. "Home Page." Accessed May 8, 2025. https://www.strose.edu.

4   Niehaus, Mary. "University of Cincinnati Co-Op: 100 Years of Success." *UC Magazine*. Accessed May 8, 2025. https://magazine.uc.edu/issues/1205/success1.html.
5   Wikipedia contributors. "Herman Schneider." Wikipedia, The Free Encyclopedia. Last modified March 4, 2025. https://en.wikipedia.org/w/index.php?title=Special:CiteThisPage&page=Herman_Schneider&id=1278739107&wpFormIdentifier=titleform.
6   WACE Inc. "Home Page." Accessed May 8, 2025. https://waceinc.org.
7   Hanson, Melanie. "Student Loan Debt Statistics." Education Data Initiative. Last modified March 16, 2025. https://educationdata.org/student-loan-debt-statistics.
8   US Department of Labor. "Fact Sheet #71: Internship Programs Under the Fair Labor Standards Act." Last modified January 2018. https://www.dol.gov/agencies/whd/fact-sheets/71-flsa-internships.
9   Hurtado, Kaitlin. "Internships for Credit: What You Need to Know." Study in the USA. October 25, 2021. https://www.studyusa.com/en/a/2064/internships-for-credit-what-you-need-to-know.
10  National Association of Colleges and Professors. "Internships." NACE. Accessed May 8, 2025. https://www.naceweb.org/tag/internships.
11  US National Science Foundation. "NSF Research Experiences for Undergraduates." Accessed May 8, 2025. https://www.nsf.gov/funding/initiatives/reu.
12  Rix, Kate. "How Undergraduates Benefit from Doing Research." U.S. News. September 27, 2023. https://www.usnews.com/education/best-colleges/articles/how-undergraduates-benefit-from-doing-research.
13  Council of Undergraduate Research. "Home Page." Accessed May 8, 2025. https://www.cur.org.
14  Society for Neuroscience. "Home Page." Accessed May 8, 2025. https://www.sfn.org.
15  Faculty for Undergraduate Neuroscience. "Home Page." Accessed May 8, 2025. https://www.funfaculty.org.
16  National Archives. "Morrill Act (1862)." Last modified May 10, 2022. https://www.archives.gov/milestone-documents/morrill-act.
17  AmeriCorps. "Home Page." Accessed May 8, 2025. https://www.americorps.gov.
18  Jacoby, Barbara, and Associates. *Service Learning in Higher Education: Concepts and Practices*. Jossey-Bass Publishers, 1996.

19. The Corella & Bertram F. Bonner Foundation. "Home Page." Accessed May 8, 2025. https://www.bonner.org.
20. The Corella & Bertram F. Bonner Foundation. "Community-Engaged Learning." Accessed May 8, 2025. https://www.bonner.org/community-engaged-learning.
21. Strom, Stephanie. "Does Service Learning Really Help?" *The New York Times*. December 29, 2009. https://www.nytimes.com/2010/01/03/education/edlife/03service-t.html.
22. Encyclopedia of Education. "Study Abroad." Encyclopedia.com. Last modified May 5, 2025. https://www.encyclopedia.com/education/encyclopedias-almanacs-transcripts-and-maps/study-abroad.
23. Study Abroad Association. "Home Page." Accessed May 8, 2025. https://studyabroadassociation.com; CEA CAPA Education Abroad. "Home Page." CEA Study Abroad. Accessed May 8, 2025. https://www.ceastudyabroad.com.
24. International Association for Business Schools and Programs Partners. "Home Page." Accessed May 8, 2025. https://www.iabsp.org.
25. SUNY COIL. "Home Page." Accessed May 8, 2025. https://coil.suny.edu.
26. University at Albany. "Home Page." Accessed May 8, 2025. https://career.albany.edu.

## CHAPTER 2

1. Goriely, Alain. "Eighty-Six Billion and Counting: Do We Know the Number of Neurons in the Human Brain?" *Brain* vol. 148, no. 3 (March 2025): 689–691. https://doi.org/10.1093/brain/awae390.
2. Weintraub, Pam. "The Empty Brain." Aeon. May 18, 2016. https://aeon.co/essays/your-brain-does-not-process-information-and-it-is-not-a-computer.
3. Schmitter, Amy M. "Hume on the Emotions." Stanford Encyclopedia of Philosophy. 2021. https://plato.stanford.edu/entries/emotions-17th18th/LD8Hume.html.
4. Damasio, Antonio. *Descartes' Error: Emotion, Reason, and the Human Brain*. Penguin Books, 1994.
5. Kahneman, Daniel. *Thinking, Fast and Slow*. Farrar, Straus, and Giroux, 2011.
6. Holt, Jim. "Two Brains Running." *The New York Times*. November 25, 2011. https://www.nytimes.com/2011/11/27/books/review/thinking-fast-and-slow-by-daniel-kahneman-book-review.html.

7   Gladwell, Malcolm. *Blink: The Power of Thinking Without Thinking*. Back Bay Books, 2007.
8   Goodreads. "Blaise Pascal: Quotable Quotes." Accessed May 8, 2025. https://www.goodreads.com/quotes/559339-the-heart-has-its-reasons-which-reason-knows-nothing-of.
9   Gilbert, Dan. "The Surprising Science of Happiness." TED video, 20:51. February 2004. https://www.ted.com/talks/dan_gilbert_the_surprising_science_of_happiness?language=en.
10  Zak, Paul. "Trust, Morality—and Oxytocin?" TED video, 16:17. July 2011. https://www.ted.com/talks/paul_zak_trust_morality_and_oxytocin?language=en.
11  Adkins, Amy. "Millennials: The Job-Hopping Generation." Gallup. Accessed May 8, 2025. https://www.gallup.com/workplace/231587/millennials-job-hopping-generation.aspx.
12  Patkin, Abby. "Northeastern's Acceptance Rate for Boston Campus Drops to 5.2%." Boston.com. August 29, 2024. https://www.boston.com/news/schools/2024/08/29/northeasterns-acceptance-rate-for-boston-campus-drops-to-5-2/.
13  Freeland, Richard M. *Transforming the Urban University: Northeastern, 1996–2006*. University of Pennsylvania Press, 2019.
14  Stellar, Jim. "Global Institute on Experiential Education—an Intense Week." *The Other Lobe* (blog). *The Other Lobe of the Brain*. July 7, 2010. https://otherlobe.com/global-institute-on-experiential-education-%E2%80%93-an-intense-week/.
15  Blei, Daniela. "How College Admissions Hurt Intergenerational Mobility." Stanford Social Innovation Review. Fall 2020. https://ssir.org/articles/entry/how_college_admissions_hurt_intergenerational_mobility.

## CHAPTER 3

1   Callard, Felicity, and Daniel S. Margulies. "What We Talk About When We Talk About the Default Mode Network." *Frontiers in Human Neuroscience* vol. 8, no. 619 (August 2014). https://doi.org/10.3389/fnhum.2014.00619.
2   Ingvar, D. H., and G. Franzen. "Abnormalities of Cerebral Blood Flow Distribution in Patients with Chronic Schizophrenia." *Acta Psychiatrica Scandinavica* vol. 50, no. 4 (1974): 425–462. https://doi.org/10.1111/j.1600-0447.1974.tb09707.x.

3   Gusnard, Debra A., John M. Ollinger, et al. "Persistence and Brain Circuitry." *Proceedings of the National Academy of Sciences* vol. 100, no. 6 (March 2003): 3479–3484. https://doi.org/10.1073/pnas.0538050100.

4   Ascencio, Brandon, Brandy Eggan, and Jim Stellar. "Brain Networks: Blog 1—The Default Mode Network." *The Other Lobe* (blog). *The Other Lobe of the Brain*. August 8, 2020. https://otherlobe.com/brain-networks-blog-1-the-default-mode-network/.

5   NyBlom, Vanessa, and Jim Stellar. "Limbic Interactions of the Dorsal Medial Prefrontal Cortex." *The Other Lobe* (blog). *The Other Lobe of the Brain*. February 2, 2023. https://otherlobe.com/%EF%BF%BClimbic-interactions-of-the-dorsal-medial-prefrontal-cortex/.

6   Akter, Sarmin, Branden Eggan, and James Stellar. "A Constant Battle: As the Amygdala Takes on the Ventromedial Prefrontal Cortex—Blog 3." *The Other Lobe* (blog). *The Other Lobe of the Brain*. August 8, 2019. https://otherlobe.com/a-constant-battle-as-the-amygdala-takes-on-the-ventromedial-prefrontal-cortex-blog-3/.

7   Glimcher, Paul W., Ernst Fehr, et al. *Neuroeconomics: Decision Making and the Brain*. Academic Press, 2008.

8   Monda-Loiacono, Ilyssa, Golshan Aghanori, et al. "The Insular Cortex, von Economo neurons, and awareness of feelings." *The Other Lobe* (blog). *The Other Lobe of the Brain*. September 9, 2013. https://otherlobe.com/the-insular-cortex-von-economo-neurons-and-awareness-of-feelings/.

9   Damasio, Antonio. *Descartes' Error: Emotion, Reason, and the Human Brain*. Penguin Books, 1994.

10  Roelke, Debra, Harlene Goldschmidt, and Martin A. Silverman. "Sentio Ergo Cogito: Damasio on the Role of Emotion in the Evolution of the Brain." *The Psychoanalytic Quarterly* vol. 82, no. 1 (September 2017): 193–202. https://doi.org/10.1002/j.2167-4086.2013.00018.x.

11  Damasio, Antonio. *Descartes' Error: Emotion, Reason, and the Human Brain*. Penguin Books, 1994.

## CHAPTER 4

1   Lokhorst, Gert-Jan. "Descartes and the Pineal Gland." Stanford Encyclopedia of Philosophy. Last modified September 18, 2013. https://plato.stanford.edu/entries/pineal-gland/.

2   Thompson, Courtney E. "Phrenology." Carnegie Mellon University. Accessed May 8, 2025. https://ethos.lps.library.cmu.edu/article/id/482/.

3   Morin, Kristen, and Jim Stellar. "What Are Soft Skills . . . Particularly Wisdom?" *The Other Lobe* (blog). *The Other Lobe of the Brain.* August 8, 2017. https://otherlobe.com/what-are-soft-skills-particularly-wisdom/.
4   Eggan, Brandy, and Jim Stellar. "Secret Computations of the Hidden Brain 1: How Brain Reward Works and Why It Matters . . . in Higher Education." *The Other Lobe* (blog). *The Other Lobe of the Brain.* March 3, 2017. https://otherlobe.com/how-brain-reward-works-and-why-it-matters-in-higher-education/.
5   Miglioretti, Diana L., Charlotee C. Gard, et al. "When Radiologists Perform Best: The Learning Curve in Screening Mammogram Interpretation." *Radiology* vol 253, no. 3 (December 2009): 632–640. https://doi.org/10.1148/radiol.2533090070.
6   Waljee, Jennifer F., and Lazar J. Greenfield. "Aging and Surgeon Performance." *Advances in Surgery* vol. 41 (2007): 189–198. https://doi.org/10.1016/j.yasu.2007.05.012.

## CHAPTER 5

1   Klein, Raymond M. "Donald Olding Hebb." Scholarpedia. April 11, 2011. http://www.scholarpedia.org/article/Donald_Olding_Hebb.
2   Yamashita, Masahiro, Mitsuo Kawato, and Hiroshi Imamizu. "Predicting Learning Plateau of Working Memory from Whole-Brain Intrinsic Network Connectivity Problems." *Scientific Reports* vol. 5, no. 7622 (January 2015). https://doi.org/10.1038/srep07622.
3   Mercenary, Jack, and Mike Mercenary. "The OK Plateau." *Business Insider.* November 3, 2013. https://www.businessinsider.com/the-ok-plateau-2013-11.
4   Turner, Karly M., Svegborn, Anna, et al. "Opposing Roles of the Dorsolateral and Dorsomedial Striatum in the Acquisition of Skilled Action Sequencing in Rats." *Journal of Neuroscience* vol. 42, no. 10 (March 2022): 2039–2051. https://doi.org/10.1523/JNEUROSCI.
5   Foer, Joshua. *Moonwalking with Einstein: The Art and Science of Remembering Everything.* Penguin, 2011.
6   Lisman, John, György Buzsáki, et al. "Viewpoints: How the Hippocampus Contributes to Memory, Navigation and Cognition." *Nature Neuroscience* vol. 20, no. 11 (October 2017): 1434–1447. https://doi.org/10.1038/nn.4661.

## CHAPTER 6

1. Rutgers-New Brunswick School of Management and Labor Relations. "Education & Employment Research Center (EERC)." Accessed May 8, 2025. https://smlr.rutgers.edu/faculty-research-engagement/education-employment-research-center-eerc.
2. Lederman, Doug, host. "Ep. 118: Colleges' Responsiveness to the Job Market." *The Key with Inside Higher Ed* (podcast). June 18, 2024. Accessed May 8, 2025. https://www.insidehighered.com/podcasts/key-podcast/2024/06/18/ep-118-colleges-responsiveness-job-market?utm_source=Inside+Higher+Ed&utm_campaign=75be28133d-podcast_2024_0720_jobmarket&utm_medium=email&utm_term=0_1fcbc04421-75be28133d-199804225&mc_cid=75be28133d&mc_eid=56edc6b805.
3. Schwartz, Barry, and Kenneth Sharpe. *Practical Wisdom: The Right Way to Do the Right Thing*. Riverhead Books, 2011.
4. Pirsig, Robert M. *Zen and the Art of Motorcycle Maintenance: An Inquiry*. Mariner Books, 2006.

## CHAPTER 7

1. Logan, Lydia. "Investing in the Future of Work: How IBM Is Tackling the Credentials Dilemma." IBM. June 7, 2022. https://www.ibm.com/think/insights/jff-horizons-and-workforce-development.
2. College Confidential contributors. "Highest IQ Majors." College Confidential. January 2020. https://talk.collegeconfidential.com/t/highest-iq-majors/2080356.
3. Gardner, Howard. *Frames of Mind: The Theory of Multiple Intelligences*. Basic Books, 2011.
4. Daniel Goleman. "Home Page." Accessed May 8, 2025. https://www.danielgoleman.info.
5. Wolos, Jeremy. "A PhD's 'Grit' Credential Shouldn't Be Undervalued." World.edu. May 6, 2018. https://world.edu/a-phds-grit-credential-shouldnt-be-undervalued/.
6. Duckworth, Angela. *Grit: The Power of Passion and Perseverance*. Scribner, 2016.
7. Vinney, Cynthia. "Understanding the Triarchic Theory of Intelligence." ThoughtCo. Last modified July 23, 2024. https://www.thoughtco.com/triarchic-theory-of-intelligence-4172497.

8   Sternberg, Robert J. *Wisdom, Intelligence, and Creativity Synthesized*. Cambridge University Press, 2007.
9   Wikipedia contributors. "The Fat Lady Sings." Wikipedia, The Free Encyclopedia. Last modified April 3, 2025. https://en.wikipedia.org/wiki/The_Fat_Lady_Sings.
10  Center for Sympathetic Intelligence. "Home Page." Accessed May 8, 2025. http://www.thecenterforsympatheticintelligence.org.
11  Zopf, Regine, Claire Marie Giabbiconi, et al. "Attentional Modulation of the Human Somatosensory Evoked Potential in a Trial-by-Trial Spatial Cueing and Sustained Spatial Attention Task Measured with High Density 128 Channels EEG." *Cognitive Brain Research* vol. 20, no. 3 (August 2004): 491–509. https://doi.org/10.1016/j.cogbrainres.2004.02.014.
12  Kam, Ka Yee, and Dorita H.F. Chang. "Sensory Eye Dominance Plasticity in the Human Adult Visual Cortex." *Frontiers in Neuroscience* vol. 17 (August 2023). https://doi.org/10.3389/fnins.2023.1250493.
13  ScienceDirect. "Visual Cortex." Accessed May 8, 2025. https://www.sciencedirect.com/topics/neuroscience/visual-cortex.
14  Seydell-Greenwald, Anna, Katrina Ferrara, et al. "Bilateral Parietal Activations for Complex Visual-Spatial Functions: Evidence from a Visual-Spatial Construction Task." *Neuropsychologia* vol. 106 (November 2017): 194–206. https://doi.org/10.1016/j.neuropsychologia.2017.10.005.
15  Spencer, Emilee. "How to Work Best with the 4 Different Types of Learners." Atlassian. October 30, 2018. https://doi.org/10.1016/j.neuropsychologia.2017.10.005.
16  Bay Atlantic University. "Auditory Learner: Characteristics & Benefits." April 2, 2024. https://bau.edu/blog/auditory-learner/#:~:text=The%20INC%20reports%20that%20auditory,or%20improve%20your%20memory%20retention.
17  Brainscape. "Cranial Nerve Mnemonics Flashcards." Accessed May 8, 2025. https://www.brainscape.com/flashcards/cranial-nerve-mnemonics-172311/packs/490401.
18  Neuroscientifically Challenged. "2-Minute Neuroscience: Wernicke's Area." YouTube video, 1:58. March 12, 2018. https://www.youtube.com/watch?v=o3Xtiz_ikw4.
19  Duckworth, Lorna. "Musicians Found to Have 'More Sensitive Brains.'" Independent. June 17, 2002. https://www.independent.co.uk/news/science/musicians-found-to-have-more-sensitive-brains-5360670.html.

20  Ibitham, Benjamin. "Influence of Learning Styles on Academic Achievement of Chemistry Students." SSRN. October 19, 2020. https://dx.doi.org/10.2139/ssrn.3714685.
21  Mueller, Pam A., and Daniel M. Oppenheimer. "The Pen Is Mightier Than the Keyboard: Advantages of Longhand over Laptop Note Taking." *Psychological Science* vol. 25, no. 6 (2014): 1159–1168. https://doi.org/10.1177/0956797614524581.
22  Craig, Debbie I. "Brain-Compatible Learning: Principles and Applications in Athletic Training." *Journal of Athletic Training* vol. 38, no. 4 (October-December 2003): 342–349. https://pubmed.ncbi.nlm.nih.gov/16558681/.
23  Botha, Monique, Robert Chapman, et al. "The Neurodiversity Concept Was Developed Collectively: An Overdue Correction on the Origins of Neurodiversity Theory." *Autism* vol. 28, no. 6 (2024): 1591–1594. https://doi.org/10.1177/13623613241237871.
24  Baumer, Nicole, and Julia Frueh. "What Is Neurodiversity?" Harvard Health Publishing. November 23, 2021. https://www.health.harvard.edu/blog/what-is-neurodiversity-202111232645.
25  Sheng, Ellen. "Walgreens, Amazon, and Wawa Find Success with the Most-Overlooked Unemployed Worker." CNBC. May 27, 2022. https://www.cnbc.com/2022/05/27/walgreens-amazon-wawa-find-success-with-most-often-unemployed-worker.html#:~:text=Unemployment%20for%20neurodivergent%20adults%20is,of%20untapped%20labor%20market%20potential.
26  Drama-Based Pedagogy. "Great Game of Power." University of Texas. Accessed May 8, 2025. https://dbp.theatredance.utexas.edu/teaching-strategies/great-game-power.
27  Stellar, James, Chrisel Martinez, et al. *Diversity at College*. Ideapress Publishing, 2020.
28  CAST. "Universal Design for Learning Guidelines." UDL Guidelines. 2024. https://udlguidelines.cast.org.

# CHAPTER 8

1  National Center for Education Statistics. "US Education in the Time of COVID." Accessed May 8, 2025. https://nces.ed.gov/surveys/annualreports/topical-studies/covid/.

2   Vardavas, Constantine, Konstantinos Zisis, et al. "Costs of the COVID-19 Pandemic Versus the Cost-Effectiveness of Mitigation Strategies in EU/UK/OECD: A Systematic Review." *BJM Open* vol. 13, no. 10 (October 2023). https://doi.org/10.1136/bmjopen-2023-077602.
3   Donnelly, Robin, and Harry Anthony Patrinos. "Learning Loss During COVID-19: An Early Systematic Review." *Prospects* vol. 51 (October 2022): 601–609. https://doi.org/10.1007/s11125-021-09582-6.
4   Kuhfeld, Megan, Beth Tarasawa, et al. "Learning During COVID-19: Initial Findings on Students' Reading and Math Achievement and Growth." NWEA. November 2020. https://www.nwea.org/research/publication/learning-during-covid-19-initial-findings-on-students-reading-and-math-achievement-and-growth/.
5   Maldonaldo, Joana Elisa, and Kristof de Witte. "The Effect of School Closures on Standardised Student Test Outcomes." KU Leuven Department of Economics. September 2020. https://feb.kuleuven.be/research/economics/ces/documents/DPS/2020/dps2017.pdf.
6   Murni, M., M. Yeni, et al. "Difficulties of Teaching Mathematics with Distance Learning Application Systems in High Schools." *Universal Journal of Educational Research* vol. 2, no. 4 (October–December 2023): 315–324. https://files.eric.ed.gov/fulltext/ED648233.pdf.
7   Putri, Eva Kristinawati, and Dwi Anggorowati Rahayu. "Science Online Learning During the COVID-19 Pandemic: Difficulties and Challenges." *Journal of Physics Conference Series* vol. 1747, no. 1 (February 2021). 10.1088/1742-6596/1747/1/012007.
8   Patch, Will. "2021 Survey of Juniors Searching for College." Niche. May 11, 2011. https://www.niche.com/about/enrollment-insights/2021-survey-of-juniors-searching-for-college/?utm_source=NACAC%20Exchange&utm_medium=email.
9   Selingo, Jeffrey L. "The Future of Gen Z: How COVID-19 Will Shape Students and Higher Education for the Next Decade." *The Chronicle of Higher Education.* 2021. https://www.gvsu.edu/cms4/asset/F1A39576-99E9-02A5-ED9B367AC0D5BA27/thefutureofgenz_interactive.pdf.
10  Top Hat. "Lessons from a Year of Pandemic Learning: Survey of 3,052 Higher Ed Students Reveals Their Expectations for Instruction and Educational Value in the Fall 2021 Academic Term." April 30, 2021. https://tophat.com/press-releases/lessons-from-pandemic-learning-survey/.

11  AACRAO. "Impact of COVID-19 on Grading, Transcript and Commencement Practices." Last modified April 10, 2020. https://www.aacrao.org/docs/default-source/research-docs/for-members-aacrao-covid-19-grading-and-transcript-practices-impacted-by-covid-19.pdf.
12  Ryberg, Renee, and Jessica Warren. "COVID-19 Has Disrupted College Plans for Students in Households with Children." Child Trends. April 27, 2021. https://www.childtrends.org/publications/covid-19-has-disrupted-college-plans-for-students-in-households-with-children.
13  Jackson, Paul, and Victor Ortego-Marti. "Skill Loss During Unemployment and the Scarring Effects of the COVID-19 Pandemic." *Labour Economics* vol. 88 (June 2024). https://doi.org/10.1016/j.labeco.2024.102516.
14  Barshay, Jill. "Proof Points: Most College Kids Are Taking at Least One Class Online, Even Long After Campuses Reopened." The Hechinger Report. January 29, 2024. https://hechingerreport.org/proof-points-most-college-kids-are-taking-at-least-one-class-online-even-long-after-campuses-reopened/.
15  Wikipedia contributors. "Blink: The Power of Thinking Without Thinking." Wikipedia, The Free Encyclopedia. Last modified March 1, 2025. https://en.wikipedia.org/wiki/Blink:_The_Power_of_Thinking_Without_Thinking.
16  Wikipedia contributors. "Thinking, Fast and Slow." Wikipedia, The Free Encyclopedia. May 7, 2025. https://en.wikipedia.org/wiki/Thinking,_Fast_and_Slow.
17  Byom, Lindsey J., and Bilge Mutlu. "Theory of Mind: Mechanisms, Methods, and New Directions." *Frontiers in Human Neuroscience* vol. 7, no. 413 (August 2013). https://doi.org/10.3389/fnhum.2013.00413.
18  Jeon, Hyeonjin, and Seung-Hwan Lee. "From Neurons to Social Beings: Short Review of the Mirror Neuron System Research and Its Socio-Psychological and Psychiatric Implications." *Clinical Psychopharmacology and Neuroscience* vol. 16, no. 1 (February 2018): 18–31. https://doi.org/10.9758/cpn.2018.16.1.18.
19  Schwartz, Berry. "Using Our Practical Wisdom." TED video, 23:06. November 2010. https://www.ted.com/talks/barry_schwartz_using_our_practical_wisdom/transcript?subtitle=en&trigger=5s.

## CHAPTER 9

1. Aoun, Joseph E. "How Higher Ed Can Adapt to the Challenges of AI." *The Chronicle of Higher Education.* July 1, 2024. https://www.chronicle.com/article/how-higher-ed-can-adapt-to-the-challenges-of-ai?utm_source=Iterable&utm_medium=email&utm_campaign=campaign_1033477.
2. Sanchez, Olivia. "Experts Predicted Dozens of Colleges Would Close in 2023—and They Were Right." The Hechinger Report. January 12, 2024. https://hechingerreport.org/experts-predicted-dozens-of-colleges-would-close-in-2023-and-they-were-right/.
3. Georgetown University Center on Education and the Workforce. "Home Page." Accessed May 8, 2025. https://cew.georgetown.edu.
4. Georgetown University Center on Education and the Workforce. "The Great Misalignment." Accessed May 8, 2025. https://cew.georgetown.edu/cew-reports/greatmisalignment/.
5. W.E. Upjohn Institute for Employment Research. "Center for Workforce Innovation and Solutions." Accessed May 8, 2025. https://www.upjohn.org/division/center-workforce-innovation-and-solutions.
6. University of Cincinnati College of Arts and Sciences. "Co-Op, Internship, and Research Opportunities and Career Planning." Accessed May 9, 2025. https://www.artsci.uc.edu/departments/seas/undergrad-programs/internshipresearch.html.
7. Northeastern University College of Professional Studies. "About the Center." Accessed May 9, 2025. https://cps.northeastern.edu/academics/schools-centers/cfhets/about/.
8. Steinbright Career Development Center. "Find Your Professional Path." Drexel University. Accessed May 9, 2025. https://drexel.edu/scdc/; Drexel University Center for the Advancement of STEM Teaching and Learning Excellence. "Paul Harrington." Accessed May 9, 2025. https://drexel.edu/castle/participants/admin-staff/Paul-Harrington/.
9. Elon University. "Work-Integrated Learning." Center for Engaged Learning. Accessed May 9, 2025. https://www.centerforengagedlearning.org/resources/work-integrated-learning/.
10. EQT Ventures. "Founder's Story: Handshake." Medium. July 5, 2022. https://medium.com/eqtventures/founders-story-handshake-2dcad-a4c1482.

11   Lunden, Ingrid. "Handshake, a LinkedIn for University Students and Diversity, Raises $40M." TechCrunch. October 31, 2018. https://techcrunch.com/2018/10/31/handshake-a-linkedin-for-university-students-and-diversity-raises-40m-on-a-275m-valuation/.
12   Indeed. "Home Page." Accessed May 9, 2025. https://www.indeed.com/.
13   ZipRecruiter. "Home Page." Accessed May 9, 2025. https://www.ziprecruiter.com.
14   Handshake. "Home Page." Handshake. Accessed May 9, 2025. https://joinhandshake.com.
15   InStage. "Home Page." Accessed May 9, 2025. https://www.instage.io.
16   JS has used the avatar interview framework as an alternative to written quizzes he gives in his Introductory Psychology class and wrote a paper with the company for the WACE 2023 world conference. The company is developing a reflection product to help students on an internship or cooperative education experience think about what they are learning.
17   Northeastern Employer Engagement and Career Design. "Big Interview." Northeastern University. Accessed May 9, 2025. https://careers.northeastern.edu/article/big-interview/.
18   Ted. "How AI Could Save (Not Destroy) Education | Sal Khan | TED." YouTube video, 15:36. May 1, 2023. https://www.youtube.com/watch?v=h-JP5GqnTrNo.
19   iQ4. "Home Page." Accessed May 9, 2025. https://www.iq4.com.
20   Applied Cybersecurity Division/NICE. "NICE Framework Resource Center." NIST. Accessed May 9, 2025. https://www.nist.gov/itl/applied-cybersecurity/nice/nice-framework-resource-center.
21   WGU. "Empowering Lifelong Learning: Digital Wallets and Collaborative Innovation." March 22, 2024. https://www.wgu.edu/blog/digital-wallets-collaborative-innovation2403.html.
22   Wikipedia contributors. "Digital Twin." Wikipedia, The Free Encyclopedia. Last modified May 9, 2025. https://en.wikipedia.org/wiki/Digital_twin.
23   National Ocean Service. "What Is Lidar?" National Oceanic and Atmospheric Administration. Accessed May 9, 2025. https://oceanservice.noaa.gov/facts/lidar.html#:~:text=Lidar%2C%20which%20stands%20for%20Light,variable%20distances.

24  Chapple, Ron, host. "Listen In: Digital Twins Promote Beneficial Outcomes for Planning and Response." *Airplane Geeks* (podcast). August 7, 2024. Accessed May 9, 2025. https://www.nv5.com/news/solutions/airports/digital-twin-podcast-ag810/.
25  Infinite Reality. *iR Enterprise* (blog). *Infinite Reality*. Accessed May 9, 2025. https://www.theinfinitereality.com/enterprise/blog.
26  American Workforce Policy Advisory Board Digital Infrastructure Working Group. "Learning and Employment Records: Progress and the Path Forward." Commerce. September 2020. https://www.commerce.gov/sites/default/files/2020-09/LERwhitepaper09222020.pdf.
27  T3 Innovation Network. "Intro to Learning and Employment Records." LER Hub. Accessed May 9, 2025. https://www.lerhub.org/s/curators/ilr-utilities/GPRNsnPxFn3XE7Qbs.
28  National Student Clearinghouse. "Myhub." Accessed May 9, 2025. https://www.studentclearinghouse.org/solutions/myhub/.
29  Logan, Lydia. "Investing in the Future of Work: How IBM Is Tackling the Credentials Dilemma." IBM. June 7, 2022. https://www.ibm.com/think/insights/jff-horizons-and-workforce-development.
30  Credential Engine. "Home Page." Accessed May 9, 2025. https://credentialengine.org.
31  WACE Inc. "Home Page." Accessed May 9, 2025. https://www.waceinc.org. Also, JS was on the Executive Committee of WACE.
32  Pramoolsook, Issra. "Development of Cooperative and Work-Integrated Education in Thailand." *Cooperative and Work-Integrated Education in Asia* (2018). https://doi.org/10.4324/9781315402024-7.
33  Tanaka, Yasushi, and Karsten Zegwaard. *Cooperative and Work-Integrated Education in Asia: History, Present and Future Issues*. Routledge, 2018.
34  SASCE. "Home Page." Accessed May 9, 2025. https://sasce.net.
35  WIL Australia. "Home Page." ACEN. Accessed May 9, 2025. https://acen.edu.au.
36  Wikipedia contributors. "Baden-Württemberg Cooperative State University." Wikipedia, The Free Encyclopedia. Last modified May 5, 2025. https://en.wikipedia.org/wiki/Baden-Württemberg_Cooperative_State_University.
37  CEIA Inc. "Home Page." Accessed May 9, 2025. https://www.ceiainc.org.
38  CEWIL Canada. "Home Page." Accessed May 9, 2025. https://cewilcanada.ca.

39 University of Waterloo. "Funding Opportunities." Accessed May 9, 2025. https://uwaterloo.ca/hire/funding-opportunities.

40 Government of Canada. "Government of Canada Launches Student Work Placements." Canada. Last modified August 28, 2017. https://www.canada.ca/en/employment-social-development/news/2017/08/government_of_canadalaunchesstudentworkplacements.html.

41 Sattler, Peggy, Julie Peters, and Academica Group, Inc. *Work Integrated-Learning in Ontario's Postsecondary Sector: The Experience of Ontario Graduates.* Toronto: Higher Education Quality Council of Ontario, 2013. https://heqco.ca/wp-content/uploads/2020/03/WIL_Experience_ON_Graduates_ENG.pdf.

42 Academic Info. "Co-op Education: An Old Idea for Current Hard Times." Accessed May 9, 2025. https://www.academicinfo.net/paying-for-college/co-op-education-an-old-idea-for-current-hard-times.

43 Queens College. "Center for Career Engagement and Internships." Accessed May 9, 2025. https://www.qc.cuny.edu/academics/cei/.

44 CEIA Inc. "History of Cooperative Education and Internships." Accessed May 9, 2025. https://www.ceiainc.org/about/history/.

45 JAG. "Home Page." Accessed May 9, 2025. https://jag.org.

46 Stellar, Jim (host). "6.2 David Kil, Data analytics, Causal AI, and Its Application to University Experiential Education Understating of Outcomes and Potential Ranking." *ExperiencED* (podcast). April 30, 2024. Accessed May 9, 2025. https://experienced.simplecast.com/episodes/62 david-kil-data-analytics-causal-ai-and-its-application-to-university-experiential-education-understating-of-outcomes-and-potential-ranking.

## CHAPTER 10

1 Experiential Learning Institute. "What Is Experiential Learning?" Accessed May 9, 2025. https://experientiallearninginstitute.org/what-is-experiential-learning/.

2 Zilles, Karl. "Brodmann: A Pioneer of Human Brain Mapping—His Impact on Concepts of Cortical Organization." *Brain* vol. 141, no. 11 (October 2018): 3262–3278. https://doi.org/10.1093/brain/awy273.

3 Schmolesky, Matthew. "The Primary Visual Cortex." In *Webvision: The Organization of the Retina and Visual System* [*Internet*]. University of Utah Health Sciences Center, 2005. Last modified June 14, 2007.

4   Basso, Michele A., and Paul J. May. "Circuits for Action and Cognition: A View from the Superior Colliculus." *Annual Review of Vision Science* vol. 3 (September 2017): 197–226. https://doi.org/10.1146/annurev-vision-102016-061234.
5   Shao, Yuxin, Caixuan Wang, et al. "ChatGPT and the Model Behind." Medium. February 10, 2023. https://medium.com/sfu-cspmp/chatgpt-and-the-model-behind-1b70022c5e29.
6   Von Stein, Kassie, and Jim Stellar. "Symbolic Representation in the Neocortex: What Is It About the 6-Layers and Their Connections That Makes the Neocortex Able to Do Symbolic Representation." *The Other Lobe* (blog). *The Other Lobe of the Brain*. December 12, 2023. https://otherlobe.com/papers/1414/.
7   Momodu, Onoseta, Vanessa NyBlom, et al. "Symbolic Representation in the Neocortex: Which Brain Areas Represent Which Limbic Processes and How Do They Work Together?" *The Other Lobe* (blog). *The Other Lobe of the Brain*. June 6, 2024. https://otherlobe.com/papers/1488/.
8   *The Other Lobe* (blog). *The Other Lobe of the Brain*. Accessed May 9, 2025.
9   Yurgelun-Todd, Deborah. "Emotional and Cognitive Changes During Adolescence." *Current Opinion in Neurobiology* vol. 17, no. 2 (April 2007): 251–257. https://doi.org/10.1016/j.conb.2007.03.009.
10  Swartz, Johnna R., Melisa Carrasco, et al. "Age-Related Changes in the Structure and Function of Prefrontal Cortex–Amygdala Circuitry in Children and Adolescents: A Multi-Modal Imaging Approach." *NeuroImage* vol. 86 (February 2014): 212–220. https://doi.org/10.1016/j.neuroimage.2013.08.018.
11  Salzman, C. Daniel, and Stefano Fusi. "Emotion, Cognition, and Mental State Representation in Amygdala and Prefrontal Cortex." *Annual Review of Neuroscience* vol. 33 (June 2011): 173–202. https://doi.org/10.1146/annurev.neuro.051508.135256.
12  Biello, David. "Fact or Fiction? Archimedes Coined the Term 'Eureka!' in the Bath." *Scientific American*. December 8, 2006. https://www.scientificamerican.com/article/fact-or-fiction-archimede/.
13  Schwartz, Barry, and Kenneth Sharpe. *Practical Wisdom: The Right Way to Do the Right Thing*. Riverhead Books, 2011.

## CHAPTER 11

1. Conzelmann, Johnathan G., Steven W. Hemelt, et al. "How Higher Education Responds to Labor Market Demand." *Employment Research* vol. 31, no. 2 (April 2024): 1–4. https://doi.org/10.17848/1075-8445.31(2)-1.
2. Conzelmann, Johnathan G., Steven W. Hemelt, et al. *Skills, Majors, and Jobs: Does Higher Education Respond?* Upjohn Institute Working Paper 24-400. Kalamazoo, MI: W.W. Upjohn Institute for Employment Research, 2024.
3. Aoun, Joseph E. *Robot-Proof: Higher Education in the Age of Artificial Intelligence*. The MIT Press, 2018.
4. National Association of Colleges and Professors. "What Is Career Readiness?" NACE. Accessed May 8, 2025. https://www.naceweb.org/career-readiness/competencies/career-readiness-defined.
5. National Association of Colleges and Professors. "Competencies for a Career-Ready Workforce." NACE. Last modified April 2024. https://www.naceweb.org/docs/default-source/default-document-library/2024/resources/nace-career-readiness-competencies-revised-apr-2024.pdf?sfvrsn=1e695024_3.
6. Institute for Experiential Learning. "Home Page." Accessed May 9, 2025. https://experientiallearninginstitute.org.
7. Dey, Farouk, and Christine Y. Cruzvergara. "Evolution of Career Services in Higher Education." *New Directions for Student Services* vol. 148 (Winter 2014): 5–18. https://nacada.ksu.edu/Portals/0/Clearinghouse/advisingissues/documents/Dey%20Cruzvergara%202014.pdf.
8. Flaherty, Colleen. "Students Sound Off on Career Centers." Inside Higher Ed. November 30, 2023. https://www.insidehighered.com/news/student-success/life-after-college/2023/11/30/survey-what-college-students-want-career.
9. The Career Leadership Collective. "As of Sept 2023, Embark and NACM Are Owned by Lightcast." Accessed May 9, 2025. https://www.careerleadershipcollective.com/nacm.
10. Ezarik, Melissa. "Painting a Picture of More Student-Centric Career Services." Inside Higher Ed. December 13, 2023. https://www.insidehighered.com/news/student-success/life-after-college/2023/12/13/how-can-campus-career-centers-better-serve.

11  VanDerziel, Shawn. "The Value of Career Services." NACE. November 28, 2022. https://www.naceweb.org/career-development/organizational-structure/the-value-of-career-services/.
12  Cruzvergara, Christine, and Michael Ellison. "Four Ways to Redesign Career Services for Students of Color." Diverse Education. February 23, 2022. https://www.diverseeducation.com/opinion/article/15288900/four-ways-to-redesign-career-services-for-students-of-color.
13  University of Albany Career Association. "UAlbany Career Advisory Network." Accessed May 9, 2025. https://www.alumni.albany.edu/s/1642/bp19/interior.aspx?sid=1642&gid=2&pgid=1910.
14  Inside Higher Ed and College Pulse. *Fall 2021 Semester in Review*. United States: College Pulse, 2021. https://reports.collegepulse.com/student-voice-fall-in-review.
15  Mowreader, Ashley. "Career Prep Tip: Helping Students Find a Professional Mentor." Inside Higher Ed. February 16, 2024. https://www.insidehighered.com/news/student-success/life-after-college/2024/02/16/five-ways-provide-students-alumni-mentoring.
16  O*Net OnLine. "Home Page." Accessed May 9, 2025. https://www.onetonline.org.
17  Catherwood, Ryan. "Measuring the Success of University Career Services." LinkedIn, June 7, 2018. https://www.linkedin.com/pulse/avoiding-university-career-services-rabbit-hole-ryan-catherwood/.
18  Kim, Joshua. 2022. "Reading 'the Nineties' as a Way of Thinking About Higher Ed's Future." *Learning Innovation* (blog). Inside Higher Ed. April 12, 2022. https://www.insidehighered.com/blogs/learning-innovation/reading-'-nineties'-way-thinking-about-higher-ed's-future.
19  MIT Undergraduate Research Opportunities Program. "Home Page." Accessed May 9, 2025. https://urop.mit.edu.

## THREE FINAL REMARKS FROM THE AUTHORS

1  Lacy, Lisa. "Laundry and Dishes? Dream On, Folks." CNET. November 16, 2024. https://www.cnet.com/tech/services-and-software/ai-and-robots-that-do-your-household-chores-dream-on-folks/.

## CONCLUSION

1  Schwartz, Barry, and Kenneth Sharpe. *Practical Wisdom: The Right Way to Do the Right Thing*. Riverhead Books, 2011.

2   Pedagogy for Change. "John Dewey." Accessed May 9, 2025. https://www.pedagogy4change.org/john-dewey/.
3   AMTProductionCo. "Peter Allen—Everything Old Is New Again." YouTube video, 8:19. May 11, 2012. https://www.youtube.com/watch?v=Z9F-fI4-0RD0.

# Index

**A**
Achievement Wallet, 167
AI. *See* artificial intelligence
Allen, Peter, 220
alumni and alumni relations offices, 207–208
Amazon, 128
American Association of Collegiate Registrars and Admissions Officers, 142
AmeriCorps, 15
amygdala, 78, 189–190, 192–194
anchoring effect, 28
*Apprentice Nation* (Craig), x
Archimedes, 195–196
Aristotle, 60, 150
artificial intelligence (AI)
 brain function vs., 26, 180, 185–186
 career services office use of, 205
 college selection using, 161–162
 COVID era integration of, 141, 144, 146
 employment changes with, 43, 217
 experiential learning connections via, 209
 higher education challenges and opportunities with, 158–161, 176–177, 200–201, 205–206, 209
 knowledge accessibility via, 2
 partnerships with technology-driven companies using, 164–170

professional wisdom vs., 217
associative stage of learning, 84
auditory cortex, 123
auditory learners, 121–123, 149
Australian Collaborative Education Network, 173
autonomous stage of learning, 84
availability bias, 28
axon, 186

**B**
basal ganglia, 80–81, 125
Big Interview program, 166
biotechnology industry, 164
*Blink: The Power of Thinking Without Thinking* (Gladwell), 28
Bonner Foundation, 16
brain function
 in amygdala, 78, 189–190, 192–194
 artificial intelligence vs., 26, 180, 185–186
 in auditory cortex, 123
 in basal ganglia, 80–81, 125
 in cerebellum, 125
 default mode network and, 46–48, 50–53, 56, 86, 187–188
 experiential learning and, 179 (*see also* experiential learning)
 for explicit thinking (*see* cognitive thinking; explicit thinking)
 in frontal cortex, 48–50, 56, 180, 186 (*see also* prefrontal cortex)
 in hippocampus, 91–92, 123

241

for implicit thinking
(*see* emotional thinking;
implicit thinking)
in insula cortex, 192–193
intelligence and, 119, 134
for learning, 121–123, 125
in limbic system, 29, 32–34, 50–
56, 96, 147, 180–181, 188–194
(*see also* emotional thinking)
in motor cortex, 82–83, 125
in neocortex, 51–52, 56, 80–81, 92, 180–194, 198
neurodiversity and, 127–132, 135
neurons in (*see* neurons)
neuroplasticity of, 33–34, 62–73, 78–79, 81, 86, 91
neuroscience evolving to understand, 59–62, 73
in nucleus accumbens, 79, 189–190
in prefrontal cortex, 32, 49–50, 51, 56, 191, 193–194
professional wisdom understanding by studying, 195–196
in regions of brain, 47–48 (*see also specific regions*)
at rest, 45–46
in somatosensory cortex, 125
in striate cortex, 82
in striatum, 86–88
two minds theory on, 26–30, 180–182 (*see also* cognitive thinking; emotional thinking; explicit thinking; implicit thinking)
in visual cortex, 121, 183–184
Broca's area, 123
Brodmann, Korbinian, 183

# C

Canadian cooperative education, 174–175
*Career Arts, The* (Wildavsky), x
career services offices, 21–22, 165, 202–207, 209–210
CEIA (Cooperative Education and Internship Association), 174, 175
Center for Sympathetic Intelligence, 118
Center for Workforce Innovation and Solutions, 163
Center on Education and the Workforce (Georgetown), 163
cerebellum, 125
CEWIL (Cooperative Education and Work-Integrated Learning), 174–175
ChatGPT, 43, 146, 158, 166, 185
Chetty, Raj, 42
*Chronicle of Higher Education, The*, 141
classical conditioning, 77, 78–79
CNBC, 128
cognitive stage of learning, 84
cognitive thinking. *See also* explicit thinking
bias to, 25–26, 28–29, 96
decision making with, 27, 30–44, 51–53, 56, 191–194
emotional integration with, 26–44, 51–53, 56, 96–97, 108–111, 150–152, 181–182, 188–198, 200, 215–216
experiential learning integration with, 15, 19, 29–32, 34, 44, 96, 196–198, 200, 215–216
group-based evolution influence on, 35–36
higher education selection and, 30–33, 36–43
higher education structure and, 25–26, 28–29, 96–97, 108–111
intelligence and, 114–115, 117–119
neocortex for, 180 (*see also* neocortex)
neuroplasticity effects on, 33–34
remote learning based on, 148–149
collaborative online international learning (COIL), 20–21
college students
brain function of (*see* brain function)
COVID-19 pandemic effects on (*see* COVID-19 pandemic; remote learning)
credits earned by, 6, 10–11, 16, 19
debt for higher education, 9, 42

higher education setting for (*see* higher education)
intelligence of (*see* intelligence)
learning by (*see* experiential learning; learning)
professional wisdom development in (*see* professional wisdom)
community immersion, 19–20
"Competencies for a Career-Ready Workforce," 202
Confucius, 30
connectomics, 61
conscious brain system. *See* cognitive thinking; explicit thinking
convergence-divergence network, 53
Cooperative Education and Internship Association (CEIA), 174, 175
Cooperative Education and Work-Integrated Learning (CEWIL), 174–175
cooperative education programs, 4–9, 10, 12, 21–22, 37–41, 163, 173–175
Council on Undergraduate Research, 14
Coursera, 145
COVID-19 pandemic
  academic and professional costs of, 139–144
  deaths from, 138
  disadvantaged population more significantly affected by, 139, 140
  economic issues in, 138, 141, 143–144
  experiential learning constraints in, 138, 142–144, 147
  fighting back against effects of, 150–154
  implicit-explicit thinking integration to counter, 150–152
  implicit or emotional thinking effects of, 140, 147–150
  mental health issues with, 140
  opportunities emerging from, 154–155
  professional wisdom damage by, 147–150
  remote learning in, 137–155
  technology growth and changes in, 137–138, 139, 141, 144–146, 151–153
Credential Engine, 171
credits, 6, 10–11, 16, 19
cross-modal sensory transfer, 187

# D

Damasio, Antonio, 26–27, 53, 191
decision making
  bias in, 27–28, 63
  on career and employment, 179
  cognitive-emotional integration for, 27–28, 30–44, 51–53, 56, 191–194
  economic mobility opportunities influencing, 42–43
  group-based evolution influence on, 35–36
  on higher education, 30–33, 36–43, 109–110, 160–162, 179
  higher education ranking influencing, 39, 41–42, 161–162, 200–202
  implicit-explicit thinking integration in, 55–57
  neuroplasticity effects on, 33–34
  reward-based, 49, 51, 62–71, 73, 77–81, 87–88, 190
default mode network, 46–48, 50–53, 56, 86, 187–188
Descartes, René, 60, 191
*Descartes' Error* (Damasio), 27, 53
Dewey, John, 219
digital twins, 168–170
diverse learners
  career services office working with, 205–206
  professional wisdom cultivation with, 132–134
  supporting, 126–135, 150
*Diversity at College: Real Stories of Students Conquering Bias and Making Higher Education More Inclusive* (Stellar et al.), 130

dopamine, 51, 62–71, 73, 78, 81,
  87–88, 190
dorsolateral striatum, 86
dorsomedial prefrontal cortex, 49
dorsomedial striatum, 86–87
Drexel University, 5, 7, 21, 163, 175,
  208
Duale Hochschule Baden-Württemberg, 173–174
Duckworth, Angela, 116

E

economic issues
  cognitive-emotional integration
    on, 27–28
  COVID-19 era, 138, 141, 143–144
  economic mobility as, 42–43
Education and Employment Research Center (Rutgers),
    107, 163
electroencephalography (EEG), 61
Elon University, 163
emotional intelligence, 115, 116–117,
    118–119
*Emotional Intelligence: Why It Can Matter More Than IQ* (Goleman), 116
emotional thinking. See also implicit
    thinking
  bias with, 27–28, 63
  cognitive integration with, 26–44,
    51–53, 56, 96–97, 108–111,
    150–152, 181–182, 188–198, 200,
    215–216
  COVID-19 pandemic and remote
    learning effects on, 140,
    147–150
  decision making with, 27–28,
    30–44, 51–53, 56, 191–194
  experiential learning integration
    with, 15, 19, 29–32, 34, 44, 96,
    196–198, 200, 215–216
  frontal cortex and, 50
  group-based evolution influence
    on, 35–36
  higher education selection and,
    30–33, 36–43
  higher education structure and,
    28–29, 96–97, 108–111

intelligence and, 115, 116–117,
  118–119
limbic system for, 29, 32–34, 50–
  56, 96, 147, 180–181, 188–194
memory and, 92
neuroplasticity effects on, 33–34
employment
  AI effects on workplace and, 43,
    217
  COVID-19 pandemic effects on,
    143–144
  decision making on career and,
    179
  experiential learning similarity
    to, 3–4, 6–7, 12, 176 (see also
    experiential learning)
  government records of, 170–171,
    173, 206, 209
  higher education leading to, 2,
    77, 107, 161–177
  neurodiversity and, 128
  professional wisdom to improve
    opportunities for (see professional wisdom)
  technology-driven companies
    and, 164–170
experiential learning
  alumni connections for, 207–208
  brain function, generally, and,
    179
  career services office role in,
    21–22, 165, 202–207, 209–210
  cognitive-emotional integration
    in, 15, 19, 29–32, 34, 44, 96,
    196–198, 200, 215–216
  collaborative online international learning for, 20–21
  community immersion course
    requirements for, 19–20
  cooperative education programs
    for, 4–9, 10, 12, 21–22, 37–41,
    163, 173–175
  COVID-19 pandemic effects on,
    138, 142–144, 147
  decision making on college
    choice based on, 37–41,
    161–162
  diversity and inclusion in,
    132–134

explicit thinking improvement with, 54–55, 72
funding for, 174–175, 208–209
government support for, 172–176, 209
higher education structure and, 2–3, 16–17, 19, 21–22, 37–38, 104, 106–111
high-school level, 176
implicit-explicit thinking integration in, 54–55, 74, 95–96, 108–111
intelligence and, 132–134
internships (unpaid) for, 8, 10–12, 54, 65–67, 75–77, 132–133, 164–166
memory in, 90–91
mentoring in, 109, 167–168, 211–214
neurodiversity and, 128
overview of, 1–4, 22–23
partnerships with technology-driven companies for, 164–170, 206
professional wisdom development with, viii–xi, 1–23, 108–111, 132–134, 200–214, 216, 219–220
real-world activities in, 3–4, 6–7
service-learning as, 14–17
study abroad programs for, 17–19
technology use for, 208–210
undergraduate research for, 12–14, 104, 211–212
value of, 1–4, 75–76, 219–220
explicit thinking. *See also* cognitive thinking
definition and description of, 48, 63
experiential learning and, 54–55, 72, 74, 95–96, 108–111
higher education for, 72, 73–74, 95
implicit thinking divide with, 53–55
implicit thinking integration with, 53–57, 59, 73–74, 95–96, 108–111, 150–152, 181–182, 215–216
implicit thinking or habit evolving from, 76, 78–80, 84–88, 92–94
learning with, 76, 79–80, 82, 84–88, 92–94
professional wisdom development with, xi, 56–57, 73
remote learning based on, 148–149

## F

Faculty for Undergraduate Neuroscience, 14
Fat Lady Sings, The, 118
fear of missing out (FOMO), 27, 36
Fitts, Paul, 84
Foer, Joshua, 89–90
*Frames of Mind: The Theory of Multiple Intelligences* (Gardner), 115
Freeland, Richard, 40
Freud, Sigmund, 26
frontal cortex, 48–50, 56, 180, 186. *See also* prefrontal cortex
frontal lobe, 48, 187
functional magnetic resonance imaging (fMRI), 61
*Future of Gen Z: How COVID-19 Will Shape Students and Higher Education for the Next Decade, The*, 141

## G

Gall, Franz Joseph, 60
Gardner, Howard, 115, 132
Gates, Bill, 114
Georgetown University, 163
German cooperative education, 173–174
Gilbert, Dan, 31–32
Gladwell, Malcolm, 28, 147
glial cells, 180, 182
Glimcher, Paul, 49
Global Institute on Experiential Education, 40
Goleman, Daniel, 116
Google, 77
Google Meet, 138
Google suite, 145, 152

government
  experiential learning support by, 172–176, 209
  learning and employment records of, 170–171, 173, 206, 209
"Great Game of Power," 128–129
"Great Misalignment" report, 163
grit, 116
group work, 35–36, 151–152

# H

habit
  learning or explicit thinking evolving into, 76, 78–80, 84–88, 92–94
  memory and, 91, 92–94
  neuroplasticity and formation of, 33–34
Hamilton, Robert, 118
Handshake, 164–165, 209, 210
happiness, 30–32
Harvard University, 77, 100
Hebb, Donald, 81
heuristics, 27–28. *See also* emotional thinking
higher education
  closure of institutions for, 2, 9, 139, 160, 172
  college students in (*see* college students)
  COVID era effects on, 138–155 (*see also* remote learning)
  credits earned in, 6, 10–11, 16, 19
  decision making on, 30–33, 36–43, 109–110, 160–162, 179
  economic mobility improved by, 42–43
  employment following, 2, 77, 107, 161–177
  experiential learning in (*see* experiential learning)
  future of, 157–177, 200–201
  government support for, 170–171, 172–176
  implicit and explicit thinking in (*see* cognitive thinking; emotional thinking; explicit thinking; implicit thinking)
  inclusion of diversity in, 127–135, 150, 205–206
  intelligence and, 113–114, 116, 119
  ivory tower of, 2–3, 96–97, 104–105, 111, 131, 159, 212–214
  learning and (*see* learning)
  *in loco parentis* role of, 2
  memory and (*see* memory)
  mentors in (*see* mentors and mentoring)
  partnerships with technology-driven companies, 164–170, 206
  plasticity of, 71–73
  professional wisdom development in, vii–xii, 199–214 (*see also* professional wisdom)
  public universities in, 14
  ranking of, 39, 41–42, 161–162, 200–202
  structure of (*see* higher education structure)
  student debt for, 9, 42
  technology challenges and opportunities for, 157–162, 164–172, 176–177, 200–201, 205–206, 208–210
Higher Education Act (1965), 175
Higher Education Quality Council of Ontario, 175
higher education structure
  classroom practices in, 98, 105
  cognitive-emotional thinking integration in, 96–97, 108–111
  cognitive thinking bias in, 25–26, 28–29, 96
  disciplinary knowledge and, 98–99
  experiential learning and, 2–3, 16–17, 19, 21–22, 37–38, 104, 106–111
  inclusive and adaptive, 127–135, 150, 205–206
  as ivory tower, 2–3, 96–97, 104–105, 111, 131, 159, 212–214
  for professional wisdom development, 95–111
  professors in, 97–105, 111, 211–214
  testing in (*see* tests and testing)
  transition vs. tradition in, 105–106

hippocampus, 91–92, 123
Hippocrates, 60
homeostasis, 180
Hume, David, 26

**I**
IBM, 114, 171, 205
implicit thinking. *See also* emotional thinking
  bias with, 63
  changing to better outcomes with, 67–71
  COVID-19 pandemic and remote learning effects on, 140, 147–150
  default mode network and, 48, 51, 53, 56
  definition and description of, 48, 63
  dopamine effects on, 51, 62–71
  experiential learning and, 54–55, 74, 95–96, 108–111
  explicit thinking divide with, 53–55
  explicit thinking integration with, 53–57, 59, 73–74, 95–96, 108–111, 150–152, 181–182, 215–216
  explicit thinking or learning evolving into, 76, 78–80, 84–88, 92–94
  frontal cortex and, 49–50
  habit with, 76, 78–80, 84–88, 91, 92–94
  higher education for, 72, 73–74, 95
  limbic system for, 50–56
  neuroplasticity and, 62–71
  professional wisdom development with, xi, 56–57, 73
  recognizing positive rewards with, 62–67
Indeed, 164–165, 209
Ingvar, David, 46, 56
Inside Higher Ed, 107, 203–204
InStage, 165–166, 210
Institute for Experiential Learning, 202
insula cortex, 192–193

intelligence
  brain function and, 119, 134
  definition and description of, 114–119
  diversity and neurodiversity altering perceptions of, 127–135
  emotional, 115, 116–117, 118–119
  experiential learning and, 132–134
  higher education and, 113–114, 116, 119
  learning and, 119–132, 134–135
  multiple types of, 115, 132
  professional wisdom and, 132–134
  sympathetic, 118
  triarchic theory of, 117–118
intelligence quotient (IQ) tests, 114–115, 117–118, 127
internships, 8, 10–12, 54, 65–67, 75–77, 132–133, 164–166. *See also* cooperative education programs; experiential learning
interpersonal learners, 125–126
interview preparation, 165–166, 170, 210
intrapersonal learners, 126
intuitive thinking. *See* emotional thinking; implicit thinking
iQ4, 166–168, 170, 209, 210
IQ (intelligence quotient) tests, 114–115, 117–118, 127

**J**
Jacoby, Barbara and Associates, 15
Jamboard, 152
Jobs, Steve, 114
Jobs for America's Graduates (JAG), 176

**K**
Kahneman, Daniel, 27–29, 36, 44, 63, 73, 147, 181, 190–191
Kahoot!, 152
Khan Academy, 145, 166
kinesthetic learners, 123–125
Kolb, David, 202

## L

*Lady Windermere's Fan* (Wilde), xii
language, inclusive, 130
Lauren, Ralph, 114
learning
    auditory, 121–123, 149
    diversity and neurodiversity effects on, 126–135 (*see also* diverse learners)
    experiential (*see* experiential learning)
    explicit thinking for, 76, 79–80, 82, 84–88, 92–94
    government records of, 170–171, 173, 206, 209
    habit or implicit thinking evolved from, 76, 78–80, 84–88, 92–94
    intelligence and, 119–132, 134–135
    interpersonal or social, 125–126
    intrapersonal, 126
    kinesthetic, 123–125
    logical, 125
    memory and styles of, 122–126
    memory distinction from, 88–92
    memory integration with, 92–94
    motor, 82–85, 86
    musical, 126
    neuroplasticity and, 33–34, 68–71, 78–79, 81, 86
    perceptual, 81–82, 89
    phases of, 84
    professional wisdom as ally of, 216
    reading/writing, 125
    relational, 93–94
    remote (*see* remote learning)
    stimulus-response, 77–81
    styles of, 119–126, 149–150
    types of, 77–85
    visual, 121
Learning and Employment Record (LER), 170–171, 173, 206, 209
Light Detection and Ranging (LiDAR), 168–170
limbic system, 29, 32–34, 50–56, 96, 147, 180–181, 188–194. See also emotional thinking
LinkedIn, 164–165, 203
logical learners, 125
Lowndes, Robert, 37

## M

Maciejewska, Joanna, 217
Massachusetts Institute of Technology (MIT), 13, 211
Mayer, John D., 116
memory
    learning distinction from, 88–92
    learning integration with, 92–94
    learning styles and, 122–126
    limbic system for, 51
    neuroplasticity and formation of, 33–34, 91
    technology effects on, 90
memory plateau, 83–85
mental health issues, 140
Mentimeter, 152
mentors and mentoring
    by alumni, 207–208
    digital, 166
    dopamine and reaction to, 66–67
    in experiential learning, 109, 167–168, 211–214
    by faculty, 14, 100, 207, 211–214
    group interactions and, 36
    for neurodivergent employees, 128
    remote learning and, 154
Merck & Co., 205
Miglioretti, Diana, 68
Miro, 152
mirror neurons, 83, 147–148
MIT (Massachusetts Institute of Technology), 13, 211
mnemonic devices, 122
*Moonwalking with Einstein* (Foer), 89
Morrill Act (1862/1890), 14
motor cortex, 82–83, 125
motor learning, 82–85, 86
musical learners, 126

## N

National Association of Colleges and Employers (NACE), 12, 202
National Initiative for Cybersecurity Education (NICE), 167–168
National Science Foundation, US, 12
National Student Clearinghouse, 171
neocortex. *See also* frontal cortex; prefrontal cortex
  brain function in, 51–52, 56, 80–81, 92, 180–194, 198
  cortical columns in, 182–186
  limbic system (cognitive-emotional) integration with, 51, 188–194
  memory in, 92
  re-representation in, 51–52, 56, 189, 198
  symbolic logic in, 180–182, 184–185, 190
  transcortical connection in, 80–81, 186–188, 191–194
neurodiversity, in learners, 127–132, 135
neurological function. *See* brain function
neurons
  computer-simulated, 185
  default mode network of, 46–48, 50–53, 56, 86, 187–188
  in limbic system, 51
  mirror, 83, 147–148
  in neocortex (*see* neocortex)
  neuroplasticity of, 33, 62, 81, 86 (*see also* neuroplasticity)
  neuroscience evolution to understand, 61
  number and interactions of, 26, 33
  von Economo, 50, 53
neuroplasticity
  for changing to better outcomes, 67–71
  higher education plasticity and, 71–73
  implicit thinking and, 62–71

learning and, 33–34, 68–71, 78–79, 81, 86
  memory and, 33–34, 91
  for recognizing positive rewards, 62–67
  synaptic, 78, 81
neuroscience, evolution of, 59–62, 73
neurotransmitters, 61, 73. *See also* dopamine
NICE (National Initiative for Cybersecurity Education), 167–168
Northeastern University
  applicants and admission to, 36–41
  experiential learning at, 5–6, 7, 21–22, 132–133, 163, 166, 175, 208
  ranking of, 39, 42
  technology use at, 166, 208
note-taking, 124–125
nucleus accumbens, 79, 189–190

## O

object permanence, 184
occipital lobe, 184
O*NET, 209
online education. *See* remote learning
operant conditioning, 77–78, 79–81
orientation leadership, 16
Other Lobe of the Brain, The, 190
oxytocin, 35–36

## P

parietal lobe, 121, 125, 187
partnerships with technology-driven companies, 164–170, 206
Pascal, Blaise, 29, 59, 215
Pavlov, Ivan, 77
peer advisors, 204
peer review, 152–153
peer tutoring, 16
perceptual learning, 81–82, 89
phrenology, 60
Pirsig, Robert M., xii, 109, 196
positron emission tomography (PET), 61
Posner, Michael, 84

*Practical Wisdom* (Schwartz and Sharpe), 108, 196, 219
prefrontal cortex, 32, 49–50, 51, 56, 191, 193–194
premotor cortex, 83
primary motor cortex, 82–83
professional wisdom
   brain function and (*see* brain function)
   COVID-19 pandemic effects on (*see* COVID-19 pandemic; remote learning)
   definition and description of, vii, 96
   higher education role in, vii–xii, 199–214 (*see also* higher education)
   higher education structure for, 95–111
   importance of developing, vii–xii, 199
   intelligence and (*see* intelligence)
   learning for developing (*see* experiential learning; learning)
professors, 97–105, 111, 211–214
public universities, 14

# Q
Queens College, CUNY, 40, 175

# R
Raichle, Marcus, 46–47
rational thinking. *See* cognitive thinking; explicit thinking
Ray, Rachael, 114
reading/writing learners, 125
reflection, 8, 10–11, 15, 166, 198, 214
relational learning, 93–94
remote learning
   academic and professional costs of, 139–144
   COVID-era effects of, 137–155
   disadvantaged population more significantly affected by, 139, 140
   experiential learning constraints with, 138, 142–144, 147
   fighting back against effects of, 150–154
   group work in, 151–152
   implicit-explicit thinking integration to balance, 150–151
   implicit or emotional thinking effects of, 140, 147–150
   learning style and, 124, 149–150
   mental health issues with, 140
   opportunities with, 154–155
   peer review in, 152–153
   professional wisdom damage by, 147–150
   technology for, 137–138, 139, 141, 144–146, 151–153
research
   professors' focus on, 99–104, 105, 111
   undergraduate, 12–14, 104, 211–212
reward pathway, 49, 51, 62–71, 73, 77–81, 87–88, 190
Rutgers University, 107, 163

# S
Salovey, Peter, 116
SASCE (Southern African Society for Co-operative Education), 173
Schneider, Herman, 4–5
Schultz, Wolfram, 64, 78
Schwartz, Barry, 108, 150, 196, 219
semantic information, 91
service-learning, 14–17
Sharpe, Kenneth, 108, 150, 196, 219
Singer, Judy, 127
Skinner, B. F., 77
Slack, 152
social learners, 125–126
social media, 145
Society for Neuroscience, 14
somatosensory cortex, 125
Southern African Society for Co-operative Education (SASCE), 173
State University of New York, 20. *See also* University of Albany, SUNY
Sternberg, Robert, 117–118
stimulus-response learning, 77–81
striate cortex, 82
striatum, 86–88

students. *See* college students
study abroad programs, 17–19
*Stumbling on Happiness* (Gilbert), 31–32
superior colliculus, 184
sympathetic intelligence, 118
synaptic plasticity, 78, 81

**T**

T3 Innovation Network, 170
TACE (Thai Association of Cooperative Education), 173
Target, 205
Teams, 138
technology
  adaptive, 131, 145–146
  AI (*see* artificial intelligence)
  career services office use of, 205–206, 210
  college selection using, 160–162
  COVID era growth and changes in, 137–138, 139, 141, 144–146, 151–153
  experiential learning connections via, 208–210
  higher education challenges and opportunities with, 157–162, 164–172, 176–177, 200–201, 205–206, 208–210
  memory affected by, 90
  partnerships with technology-driven companies, 164–170, 206
temporal lobe, 123
temporo-parietal-occipital junction, 48, 56
tests and testing
  credit via, 6
  diversity of options for, 131
  of experience and skill, 22, 31, 71, 91
  of intelligence, 114–115, 117–118, 127
  memorization for, 34, 71, 88–89, 91, 96
  professors' approach to, 98, 103
  remote learning and, 149
  standardized, in COVID era, 140–141
  technology effects on, 158–159

Thai Association of Cooperative Education (TACE), 173
thalamus, 183
theory of mind, 147
*Thinking, Fast and Slow* (Kahneman), 27–28, 63
trajectory concept, 184–185
transcortical connections, 80–81, 186–188, 191–194
*Transforming the Urban University* (Freeland), 40
Trello, 152
triarchic theory of intelligence, 117–118

**U**

UAlbany Career Advisory Network (UCAN), 207–208
uncinate fasciculus, 193–194
unconscious brain system. *See* emotional thinking; implicit thinking
undergraduate research, 12–14, 104, 211–212
Undergraduate Research Opportunities Program (UROP), 13, 211
Universal Design for Learning, 130–131
University of Albany, SUNY, 21–22, 40, 207–108
University of Cincinnati, 4–5, 21, 163, 175, 208
Upjohn Institute for Employment Research, 163, 200
USA Memory Championship, 89
US Census Bureau, 143
*US News & World Report* college ranking, 39, 41–42

**V**

Van Noy, Michelle, 107
ventral premotor cortex, 83
ventromedial prefrontal cortex, 49, 191
virtual education. *See* remote learning
visual cortex, 121, 183–184
visual learners, 121
von Economo neurons, 50, 53

## W

WACE (World Association of Cooperative Education), 5, 173, 175
Walgreens, 128
Walmart, 205
Waterloo University, 166, 174
Wawa, 128
Webex, 138
Wernicke's area, 123
Western Governors University, 167
W. E. Upjohn Institute for Employment Research, 163, 200
white matter connections, 186–188, 193–194
Wikipedia, 145
Wilde, Oscar, xii, 96
World Association of Cooperative Education (WACE), 5, 173, 175

## Y

YouTube, 145

## Z

Zak, Paul, 36
*Zen and the Art of Motorcycle Maintenance* (Pirsig), xii, 109, 196
ZipRecruiter, 165, 209
Zoom, 138, 151–153, 159, 167
Zuckerberg, Mark, 114